WOMBAT IN THE WILD

'Hilda said Batty can dig his own roots and stuff. Maybe that's the answer!' declared Mandy.

'Meaning what?' Gary looked puzzled.

'Well, maybe we've been on the wrong track, trying to find Batty a good home and not getting anywhere. Wombats really belong in the great outdoors, don't they?'

'Right!' Gary began to see what she was getting at.

Mandy stroked Batty's head and gazed out from the loft. 'And if he's half-wild already, why stick him in a yard in the town somewhere? Why don't we do the opposite? We could put Batty back into the wild!'

Animal Ark series

LUCY DANIELS

Wombat
— *in the* —
Wild

Illustrations by Shelagh McNicholas

*Hodder
Children's
Books*

a division of Hodder Headline plc

Special thanks to Jenny Oldfield
Thanks also to veterinarian Bairbre O'Malley for reviewing the
information contained in this book.

Text copyright © 1996 Ben M. Baglio
Created by Ben M. Baglio
London W6 0HE

First published in Great Britain in 1996
by Hodder Children's Books

The right of Lucy Daniels to be identified as the Author of the Work
has been asserted by her in accordance with the Copyright, Designs
and Patents Act 1988.

A Catalogue record for this book is available from the British Library

ISBN 0 340 65580 1

Typeset by Avon Dataset Ltd, Bidford-on-Avon, Warks

Printed and bound in Great Britain by
Cox & Wyman Ltd, Reading, Berks

Hodder Children's Books
a division of Hodder Headline plc
338 Euston Road
London NW1 3BH

One

'No worries!' Graham Masters told Mandy Hope. He'd driven to Mitchell Gap from his animal rescue centre at Peppermint Hill. There was an injured young kangaroo in the back of his Landcruiser. 'But I need a vet to take a look at this little joey. There's no rush. She's bedded down nice and cosy back there. I reckon we'll just wait our turn.'

'You're sure she's not an emergency?' Mandy pulled her bush-hat firmly down over her forehead to shield her face from the hot summer sun. It was coming up to Christmas, the time of year when the temperatures soared in Eurabbie

Bay, on the east coast of Australia. She peered into the back of the rescue pick-up. The young joey was fast asleep, front paws curled underneath her chin. Mandy turned to Graham. 'How old is she?' she whispered.

'I'd say eight or nine months, nearly too big to ride in the mother's pouch. I found her all alone and crook, by a stream down by the bay. I reckon she got cut off from the rest of the mob. It looks like a dingo has had a go at her.'

'Poor thing!' Mandy gazed at the sleeping kangaroo. 'Where's she hurt?'

'Her ear got chewed right here, see.' Gently Graham bent over the side of the pick-up and stroked the kangaroo's head. 'She's lost a bit of blood, needs a couple of stitches, then she'll be right.' He stood back, hands in pockets, and squinted up at the sun.

Mandy followed him on to the shaded veranda of their white surgery building. The Hopes had been at Mitchell Gap for just two months. They'd swapped places with the Munroes, an Australian family. New South Wales for North Yorkshire, Eurabbie Bay for Welford. For a whole six months they'd left Animal Ark to live and work at Mitchell Gap.

The exchange was working out well. Though Mandy sometimes felt homesick, and though she missed Gran and Grandad Hope, her best friend, James Hunter, and all the kittens, puppies, goats and hedgehogs she'd helped at Animal Ark, she knew she'd be back there soon. Meanwhile she was having a terrific time down under!

The animals here were fascinating. For instance, the fact that a kangaroo carried her young in a pouch, like a built-in purse, was amazing.

Mandy thought of the injured youngster in the back of the Landcruiser. 'What will happen to her after she's treated? Will she be able to go straight back to her mother?'

Graham nodded. He lifted his hat and ran a hand through his wavy brown hair. 'The sooner the better, I reckon. I plan to take her back to where I found her right after they've taken a look at her here. You want to come?'

Mandy jumped at the chance. 'When?'

'After you're through with surgery.'

Mandy dashed into the air-conditioned reception room where Katie, their young, energetic nurse, ticked off appointments in the book. The room was crowded with the usual mixture of cats and dogs, plus a pet snake and a cockatoo. 'Katie, do you think you'll need me after surgery?' she asked. She often helped to clean out the consulting rooms.

Katie smiled. 'No. But didn't I hear that Gary was coming across?'

Gary Simpson lived at Waratarah, a large house on top of the hill, where Katie herself stayed as a lodger. Gary and Mandy were already firm friends. He'd always been sports mad, but just now he seemed to be making time to follow up a sudden interest in animals. Katie said with a wink that it was since Mandy had arrived at Mitchell Gap. And he also spent hours teaching Mandy to boogie board; easier than surfing, but with all the thrill of the crashing waves and foaming surf.

'Oh yes, that's right!' Mandy remembered that she'd fixed a boogie boarding session with him. 'Do you think Gary would mind making a detour to help Graham take a joey back into the bush?'

'Why not ask him?' Katie pointed through the open door.

Gary had just cycled across the yard and flung his bike down against the veranda. He leaped up the three steps and swung into the reception room, whistling and looking round for Mandy. 'G'day!' he grinned. His curly fair hair and grey eyes set off a deep summer tan. He wore a white T-shirt over bright blue shorts and bare feet.

'Hi!' Mandy grinned back. She'd picked up a deep tan herself, and taken to the local kids' style of going around in a T-shirt and shorts. She wore her blonde hair in a high ponytail to stay cool. 'Come outside a second. There's something you might like to see!'

Katie winked knowingly.

Mandy ignored her. 'Gary, Graham's brought in this gorgeous joey. She's in the pick-up. Come and see.' She expected him to be won over the moment he set eyes on the young kangaroo. 'What do you think?'

He nodded. 'Pretty good.' He didn't go in for long-winded replies.

'A dingo chewed her ear, look.'

'You gonna fix it?'

'No worries,' Mandy assured him. 'Do you want to help Graham put her back in the bush afterwards? You could leave your bike and Graham can drop us off at the beach after we've set her free.'

'Sounds good.'

'Great.' Mandy was happy. They went inside, and she began to whizz through her jobs. She fed a greyhound who was staying with them in the unit, then groomed a pony from the riding-school in Eurabbie. The pony had breathing problems, possibly connected with the type of hay he was being fed. Emily Hope had brought him into the surgery for observation. He was a sweet-tempered grey with gentle, dark eyes and a long white mane. Mandy talked softly to him as she brushed and combed. Then she turned him out into a small paddock by the stream where a family of platypuses had made their burrow.

Mandy stopped to study the clear water. There was no sign of the platypuses in the afternoon heat so she went back into the surgery, just in time to watch her dad inject the joey with a local anaesthetic. He put four stitches into the jagged tear in her soft, pointed ear, working quickly and neatly. He talked to his patient in a soothing voice, making sure that the kangaroo felt no pain. Soon he had finished, and the joey was twitching her nose at the strange medical smells all around. She was clearly anxious to be off.

'There you go, fit as a fiddle,' Adam Hope said. 'Those stitches will dissolve when they've done their job. She should be as right as rain in a few days.'

Graham Masters gave a satisfied nod. 'Time to get her back to her mum.' He scooped the kangaroo into his strong arms. 'Those look like pretty good stitches to me,' he said.

'The anti-tetanus jab, plus an antibiotic, will stop infection,' Mandy's dad assured him. 'I hear you're planning to drop her back where you found her. Will the mother come looking, or will she have to fend for herself from now on?'

'No, the mother will come. They stick together, these roos. In fact, she's probably there right now, wondering where the little mite's got to.' He nodded at Mandy and Gary to follow him quickly.

'See you later.' Mr Hope gave them a wave from the veranda. 'Do you want me to drive down to pick you up?'

Mandy climbed into the back of the Landcruiser. 'Yes, please!'

'Where shall we meet?'

'At the beach!' she yelled, then waved as the pick-up rolled slowly out of the gate. Dust rose from beneath the crunching wheels.

'Where else?' Mr Hope smiled. Not a single long summer day went by without a visit to the surfing paradise. He turned and went inside, as Graham drove them down the steep hill towards the sparkling blue ocean.

They set the joey free by a creek in the valley to the north of Eurabbie Bay. The little kangaroo raised herself on strong hind legs. Her nose twitched. The air was heavy with the scent of acacia blossom and gum trees. In a field across the creek, a herd of black and white dairy cows munched contentedly. It was only when she looked carefully that Mandy spotted the bunch of grey kangaroos gathered quietly in the shade of the tall gum trees, patiently waiting.

'Over there!' She pointed.

Graham picked up the joey then strode ahead through the clear shallow stream, carrying the young roo against his shoulder. Mandy and Gary followed close behind. A magpie shrieked a warning from high in the trees.

The half dozen female kangaroos raised their heads and sniffed the air. Graham lowered the joey safely to the ground. 'I reckon that's her

mum at the front of the clan,' he told the others.

They watched as one kangaroo broke free and came towards them. She stopped and bent low, making small clucking sounds in the back of her throat. Then she beckoned with her small black hand, called again, louder this time. She gave a short, deep cough that seemed to mean, 'Come here at once!'

At last the joey spotted her through the tall dry grass. The youngster took one final look at Graham over her shoulder, then coughed out a reply. Mandy laughed at the deep rough sound coming from such a small pretty creature. She saw the joey set off with a sudden leap. Three bounds and she was safe with her mother.

'Hmm,' Graham grunted and smiled.

The mother sniffed hard and licked her joey's injured ear. In response, the baby climbed straight into the pouch. Two other females came close to the water's edge, out of the shade. They reared up, sniffed, listened and looked, alert to the possible dangers of dingoes, eagles, even dogs. Mandy saw that one had a tiny baby peering out of her own pouch.

Then the whole group re-formed by the stream, gathering in the hazy heat, sending blue

and red butterflies fluttering high overhead.
They came close to Mandy, Gary and Graham.
Mandy could almost have reached out and
touched them as they loped lazily by, heading
for fresh shade and new grass to graze.

The injured joey was safely back with her clan,
thanks to Graham.

'Catch you later,' he said under his breath to
the mob of kangaroos. He watched them bound
across the sun-scorched earth. 'Come on, mates,'
he said to Mandy and Gary. 'Let's get down to
that beach!'

Two

It was late in the afternoon when Mandy's dad turned up to fetch them from Two People Beach in Eurabbie Bay. This was the favourite surfing beach; a lonely, horseshoe-shaped cove sheltered by cliffs, where the water crashed against the white sand and surfers rode the waves.

Mandy and Gary had joined the gang after being dropped off by Graham. Their friends, Dean and Suzi Peratinos, were already boogie boarding. Soon Julie, the junior champion, came along too. They spent a glorious hour riding the breakers.

'Can you bear to tear yourselves away?' Adam

Hope asked. 'Or should I come back again later?' He glanced at his watch, standing with his arms folded, ankle-deep in the soft, warm sand.

Mandy shook the salt water out of her hair. She'd jogged up from the water's edge, her board tucked under one arm. 'Why, where are we going next?'

'I have to call in at Hilda Harris's farm on the far side of Peppermint Hill.'

'That's on the way home, isn't it?' She realised that it would mean extra driving for her dad if she chose to hang on here. 'I'd better come now. I'll just see what Gary wants to do.' She trotted down to the sparkling shoreline to fix things up with her friend. Then she ran back up the beach alone. 'Gary wants to stick around a bit longer. Dean's dad will be along to give them all a lift home.'

'Fine.' Mr Hope smiled. He took a towel from his shoulder and handed it to her. 'Give me the board. Let's get a move on.' Together they headed up the steep cliff path towards the red Landcruiser parked at the top. 'Hilda reckons she's got a couple of cows due for vaccination,' he told Mandy. 'I said I'd call in around five.'

She nodded, enjoying the breeze against her tingling face as they set off towards Peppermint Hill. 'I didn't know she kept cows.'

'Oh, Hilda's got a couple of everything; goats, chickens, sheep. Orchard Farm's a homely little place tucked away by a creek, surrounded by apple orchards. It's like a smallholding back home, except that it's sunny!'

Mandy grinned. 'I know. I've been there.'

'When?' Her dad pulled off the main road, down a bumpy track. They drove deep into a steep-sided valley, where the hillsides were white with blossom.

'When we first arrived at Mitchell Gap. Mum had to come out to look at Moses, Hilda's old tom-cat.' Moses had used up another of his nine lives in a fight with a kangaroo. The roo had given him a hefty kick and left his ribs bruised and sore. Emily Hope had checked him over and given him the all-clear.

Mandy remembered that Hilda Harris lived alone on her farm. She recognised its wobbly fences and broken-down barn door. Paint flaked from the window frames and weeds grew up through the veranda floorboards.

'Ready?' Adam Hope said, lifting his bag from

the back seat. They'd pulled up outside the front door.

At the sound of their car engine, Moses crept out through a hole in the barn door. He stalked up to Mandy, tail in the air. She bent to stroke him while her dad went to find Hilda. 'Hello, old boy.' The striped tom-cat rubbed against her legs. He looked fit again, well-fed, and a match for any kangaroo. He was strongly built, with a broad face and fine long whiskers, a real bruiser when he got into a scrap, Mandy guessed. His owner was the opposite; a tiny woman with curly white hair, who dressed in oversized men's clothes that swamped her frail figure.

Hilda Harris came out of the house with Mandy's father. She carried a glass of orange juice and home-made biscuits for Mandy. 'I already brought the girls in from the field for milking,' Hilda told Adam Hope. 'They're in the barn.'

'Thanks. I think I'll manage best by myself now,' he told them, going off to do his job of vaccinating the cows against disease.

'You want to help me feed the chooks?' Hilda pointed to the hens, then strode off in her man-sized boots.

Mandy followed. She took her lead from the

old farmer, learning how to spread grain for the hens by letting it trickle through her fingers as she threw her arm wide in a semicircle. She watched fascinated as the glossy brown hens darted at the corn with their hard, sharp beaks, their bright red combs bobbing this way and that. Over at the far side of the yard, she spotted a beehive alive with the humming of hundreds of bees busily making honey. And beyond the tumbledown fence stretched the apple trees. 'Oh!' Mandy broke off from feeding the hens. She'd caught sight of an animal steadily munching at the lush grass beneath the trees. It was a fine, fully grown black goat with white markings on her face and legs.

Hilda followed her gaze. 'Here,' she said, 'give me that.' She took the bowl of corn. 'I'll feed the chooks. You go and have a chat with Matilda.'

Mandy didn't need telling twice. Goats drew her like a magnet. She hadn't met a goat yet who didn't have personality by the sackload. They were wonderfully clever and wicked. They could outsmart any owner in their search for the best grass, the most delicious tidbit. Soon Mandy was sitting astride the fence, stroking Matilda's bony head and admiring her fine dark eyes.

'She's glad of a bit of company.' Hilda came up quietly from behind.

Mandy turned. 'Don't you have other goats?' She took a quick look round the empty orchard. It was odd to have only one, even on a small farm like this.

'Did have. Not any more.' Hilda's eyes narrowed. She turned away. 'Come on, let's see if your dad's finished with my cows yet.'

Something warned Mandy not to ask any more questions. She said a fond goodbye to Matilda and jumped down from the fence to follow Hilda towards the barn.

The old lady chatted on ten to the dozen about the heat, the storm that was brewing up for later that evening, anything except the goat's missing companions. When they reached the yard, she bent absent-mindedly to stroke old Moses. He sat in the sun by the barn door. 'Are you through yet?' Hilda called to Mr Hope.

'Give me five more minutes,' he replied.

Hilda shrugged. 'He's very thorough.' She looked closely at Mandy. 'Ever seen a wombat?' she said suddenly.

Mandy felt a tingle in the back of her neck. 'Only once close to; at Mitchell Gap. I've seen

quite a few in the wild, though, from a distance.'
She smiled at the thought of the slow, sturdy
creatures. They were one of the country's
marvels, alongside the kangaroo and the koala.
They had fat brown bodies and short legs. They
were comical creatures, with their snub noses
and friendly, round faces. She knew that a few
people kept them as pets; that was how she'd
got her close-up view of Harry, Mal Stalker's
chubby wombat, when he came into the surgery.

'Want to see another one?' Hilda's questions
were crisp and no-nonsense.

Mandy's eyes lit up. She nodded.

'Come this way.' She arched her eyebrows and
led the way down the side of the barn.

They soon came to a flight of worn wooden
steps that led to a hayloft above the barn where
Adam Hope was at work. Mandy followed Hilda
up to the airy loft, noticing that the old lady
had begun to puff and wheeze as she mounted
the stairs and flung open the rickety door.

Hilda poked her head inside. 'Batty!' she
called softly. 'Come here, mate!'

Mandy peered over her shoulder. The floor
of the loft was lined with clean straw, and the
whole place smelt of ripe, sweet apples. No

daylight entered, and it took a few seconds for Mandy's eyes to get used to the semi-darkness. But then she spotted a movement in the far corner. First there was a heavy rustling amongst a high pile of straw. Then a blunt nose appeared, and two tiny, dark eyes. The nose twitched, and the wombat backed shyly into his hiding-place once more.

'Oh, come out, Batty, no one's going to hurt you!' Hilda said sternly. She drew Mandy into the loft and closed the door. Daylight filtered in through holes in the roof. 'He's bad with strangers,' she explained, 'but friendly enough when he gets to know you.'

Mandy crouched patiently on the straw-covered boards. Once more the head appeared from the untidy pile in the corner, then two rounded ears. Hilda dug her hand deep into her trouser pocket and gave Mandy a handful of tough looking grass roots. 'Why not give him these?' she prompted.

Mandy took the roots and crept forward. This time Batty didn't retreat. She could still see his coarse brown fur, his barrel-shaped body, his sturdy, stumpy legs. 'Here, boy!'

The wombat waddled forward. He sniffed the

roots, gingerly curled his lips round them and began to chomp with his two large incisor teeth at the front of his top jaw. Mandy felt his lips tickle the palm of her hand. She murmured with delight.

'Why not give him a stroke?' Hilda looked on with a broad smile.

'Are you sure he'll let me?'

'Oh, yes. Now you've fed him, you're his friend for life!'

Mandy rubbed Batty's forehead with her knuckles, then ran her palm down the length of his back. He was similar in size and shape to a badger back home, blinking at her like a short-sighted, stout old man. He coughed. Surprised, Mandy laughed.

'Poor thing, he's not getting any younger.' Hilda smiled too, as the old wombat coughed again. 'Neither are any of us!'

'How old is he?'

'Thirteen. And he's lived here with me since he was under a year old.'

'He has a good life up here in the loft.' It was warm and clean, and cosy and dark for this night-loving chap. 'Does he ever go out?'

'Only into the yard. I carry him down, and he scratches about a bit for his own food. He doesn't like to be cooped up – likes some independence, don't you my old mate?' Hilda came and gave him a stroke. 'What do you reckon; do you think your dad will be through with Daisy and Buttercup now?' She stood straight, putting one hand to her back. 'Shall we go and see?'

Reluctantly Mandy said goodbye to Batty. 'Catch you later,' she said with the Australian twang.

The wombat grunted. He turned to burrow deep into his warm hay. 'If you're lucky,' he seemed to signal.

The last she saw of him was his broad backside and short back legs, wriggling cosily into the nest.

Out in the yard, Adam Hope was rolling down his sleeves. He reported that the two cows were both fit and healthy, then he dated and signed a form to say that he'd given them their jabs. He handed it back to Hilda. 'As a matter of fact, it's not quite run out yet,' he pointed out. 'You could've waited until after Christmas.'

'Ah.' Hilda clamped her jaw tight shut and shoved the form into her shirt pocket. 'That's where you're wrong.'

Mr Hope looked puzzled. Mandy left them to chat, and went off in search of Moses. When she came back, she saw that her dad was looking serious. Hilda stood with her back to Mandy, explaining her problems to him. 'I'm falling to bits, see, just like the old place. I reckon we're both past our sell-by dates!'

Mandy glanced at the peeling paintwork. One broken window was roughly boarded up. Apple blossom petals had shaken free and blew across the farmyard in an east wind that had suddenly got up. A door banged and rattled.

'Never!' Adam Hope put on a cheerful voice.

'Yes, yes, I'm crook, see.' She patted her chest. 'It's my old ticker. I had to promise the doc that this was my last year at Orchard Farm. He warned me I wouldn't stagger on by myself much longer, so I promised him I'd be out by Christmas!'

'But where will you go?'

'No worries.' Hilda tried to make light of things. 'I'm off to stay with my nephew and his family in Sydney.'

'In the city?'

Mandy's forehead knitted into a frown as she stood by and listened. Hilda sounded sad to be leaving, but resigned all the same. It was as if she'd had a long time to think about moving out from the place she loved.

'I've been lucky. I've lived in this beautiful valley for more than sixty years,' she told them. 'I reckon that's a pretty good innings.'

'But it must make it all the harder to leave.' Mandy's dad was full of sympathy. He looked around the ramshackle buildings, at the faded wooden farmhouse and the weed-strewn yard.

'I can't complain. But that's why I needed to get a jab for Daisy and Buttercup, see. They're moving on, over the other side of the hill to

Bill Danvers' place. He says he can take them into his dairy herd, as long as they have a clean bill of health.'

Adam Hope nodded. 'There's no problem there.' They fell into a sad silence.

This was why Matilda the goat was left all alone in the orchard, Mandy realised. There had once been other goats and farm animals around the place, but they'd already been shipped out to their new homes. 'What about Moses?' she asked.

The tom-cat came prowling along the side of the house, then darted under the veranda out of sight.

Hilda sighed. 'He can come with me to Sydney. It's all arranged. No, it's Matilda I'm worried about. Waltzing Matilda. I called her that because she's always waltzing off by herself, getting into mischief.' She turned to Mr Hope. 'Graham Masters is looking out for a new place for her, but I'd be glad if you could do the same.' She wrinkled her eyes and looked him in the face in a straight appeal.

'Course,' he nodded. 'We'll soon find somewhere. She's a fine looking goat.'

'But a bit of a handful, like I said.' It seemed

Hilda knew her animals inside out.

'Before Christmas, you say?'

'Yes, that's when I lock up the old place for the last time.'

He nodded thoughtfully. They stood outside in the rising wind. Raindrops began to splash against their faces. Mandy had one last question, but she feared the answer before she even asked. 'And what about Batty?' Her stomach tightened, her hands grew hot and sticky, as the rain began to fall in earnest. After all, who would be willing to take on a thirteen year old, shambling old wombat, quiet and set in his ways?

Mandy looked from Hilda to her dad and back again. There was no reply, and no happy ending in sight for the stout, shy creature in the hayloft.

The wind blew and the rain soaked them to the skin as they said goodbye to Hilda Harris and drove home to Mitchell Gap in a heavy silence.

Three

The sudden storm, known locally as a buster, soon blew itself out. Next morning, the skies over Mitchell Gap were clear blue, but Mandy was still troubled.

'What's up?' Emily Hope said. They were having breakfast beside the pool in their yard, watching Mandy's dad get his morning exercise. He swam up and down, making great waves as he turned and plunged into a new length.

Mandy shook her head. 'Not a lot.' She didn't want to talk about poor old Batty. Somehow talking about him would make the problem of him having nowhere to go all the worse. There was exactly a week to go until Christmas, then Hilda would pack up at Orchard Farm for good and leave for Sydney.

Her mum seemed to realise that she needed cheering up. 'Katie's taking a drive up to Graham's place at Peppermint Hill this morning. Why not go along for the ride?' Mandy wasn't her usual busy, cheerful self. It wasn't like her not to make the most of every moment of the school holidays. 'She's going to drop Tim the greyhound there. You could go up with her and take a look at Graham's menagerie.'

Slowly Mandy nodded. 'OK.' She got up to go inside for her hat and shoes. 'Do you want anything from the shop in Mitchell while we're out?'

Her mum smiled. 'No thanks. Merv's driving by this afternoon with the usual delivery.' Merv Pyke, the grumpy, middle-aged shopkeeper in Eurabbie, never missed a day. He brought fresh bread, milk and eggs to all the scattered farms and houses in the hilly country surrounding the bay.

'Oh, right.' Mandy paused in the doorway. 'Mum, can you ask if he happens to know of a good home for Hilda's goat?' Merv knew

everything that went on in Eurabbie Bay. 'You
know she has to leave Orchard Farm?'

Mrs Hope nodded. 'Your dad did mention it,
yes.' She got up and put an arm round Mandy's
shoulder. 'He also mentioned something about
a cranky old wombat.'

'Batty's not cranky, he's sweet!' she protested.
'He's just shy with strangers, that's all.'

'Is that who you're really worried about?'

Mandy nodded. 'I don't think Hilda knows
what to do with him. And what *is* going to
happen when she finally has to pack up and
leave?'

'I wonder.' Emily Hope looked thoughtful. 'I
wonder if she *has* really tried to find Batty a
good home. From what I hear, she's pretty fond
of this wombat of hers. Parting from him will
be a terrific wrench. You know, when people
don't really want to do something, often they
can't bring themselves to get properly
organised.' She let go of Mandy and wandered
into the yard. She stood there in her long white
cotton skirt and loose shirt, her red hair catching
the sunlight.

'You think she needs some help?' Suddenly
Mandy perked up.

'Well, I don't think it could do any harm.'

Mandy nodded. 'You're right, Mum. I'll mention it to Graham. Now, I'd better let Katie know I'll be coming along with her. Katie!' She ran across the yard, skirting the pool and dashing up the steps into the surgery. All her energy had come rushing back, now that her mum had suggested a plan of action.

Soon Mandy and the practice nurse were out on the road, with Tim the greyhound sitting quietly on the front seat between them. He'd been found a week earlier in an empty lock-up garage in the centre of Eurabbie. He was thin and weak when Merv found him and brought him up to Mitchell Gap. A few days of good feeding, boosted with vitamins and all the usual jabs had set him back on his feet. Now they were taking him along to Graham's place in the hope of finding him a suitable new home.

The road to the rescue centre took them past the rough turning down to Orchard Farm. Mandy felt a pang of worry for Hilda and her few remaining animals. But soon they arrived at Peppermint Hill, to a noisy row of kennels and compounds that housed all the waifs and strays in the area. They ranged from dogs like

Tim to wild wallabies and bandicoots brought in from the bush. They usually had small injuries that Graham did his best to mend. He greeted them now, as he emerged from the shady compound where he kept the lame kangaroos and wallabies.

'G'day!' He looked pleased to see them.

Mandy let Tim out of the car. They watched him sniff his way round the yard, ears pricked, head turning this way and that. Finally he trotted up to Graham, who made a great fuss of him.

'Hey, you're great!' Graham laughed as the greyhound licked his hand. 'I reckon someone will come along and take you home, no worries!'

The dog wagged his tail.

Graham led them into his untidy office. It looked not much bigger than a cupboard, with boxes and files piled on top of a tiny desk. A telephone rang from underneath a clutter of paperwork. Graham brushed everything to one side and picked up the phone. 'G'day, Peppermint Hill Rescue Centre.' He listened and jotted something down, then he grinned as he put down the phone.

'Good news?' Katie perched on the edge of the desk. She swung her legs and fanned herself with the brim of her straw hat.

'That's Jim Morris up in the hills at Shelley Ridge. He runs a goat farm. He says he's got room for Hilda Harris's tearaway, no problem. That's one less worry for her.' Graham never raised his voice or got excited, but even he sounded relieved.

'You mean Matilda?' Mandy felt a weight lift from her own shoulders.

'Yeah, good old Waltzing Matilda. I mentioned her to Merv the other day, soon as I heard Hilda was having a spot of bother finding somewhere for her to move on to. Merv gets about more than most. He can drop in a good word here and there. Eventually Jim Morris got to hear, and what do you know, I get a phone call from him asking if the goat's a good milker, and if so he'll drive over to fetch her from Hilda's place tonight. He didn't seem worried that she's got itchy feet. He's used to it, looking after forty goats of his own.'

Mandy pictured Matilda settling in at Jim Morris's place, running him round in circles, trying to get the best grass and clover, the sweetest hay. Shelley Ridge sounded ideal. 'Has Hilda managed to get all her animals sorted out now?' she asked. They wandered outside and sat in the shade of a tall mountain ash, with Tim like a grey shadow at Graham's heels.

'Yeah, except for a couple of chooks, but they're dead easy.' Graham took some gum from his top pocket and offered the packet to Katie and Mandy. 'Most people round here would be glad of a few extra chooks.'

Mandy waited for a while. 'What about Batty?' she dropped in quietly.

'Who's Batty?' He crouched with his hands clasped around his knees, watching the kangaroos in the compound.

'Didn't she mention him? He's a wombat.'

'And he needs a home?' He frowned.

'Yes. She says she can't take him with her to the city.'

'I wonder why she never asked me.'

'Mum says it's probably because she doesn't really want to part with him.'

'That'd be right,' Katie nodded. 'I've met the old cobber a couple of times; I can see why she doesn't want to let him go.'

'He's great, isn't he?' A grin flashed across Mandy's face. 'But she will have to part with him, like it or not.'

'I reckon it's not going to be quite that easy.'

'Why not?'

'Well, first off, you need a licence to keep a wombat. It's an official rule. Second, no one round here really wants one, see. Mal Stalker has a few problems keeping Harry as a pet. There's always some old farmer wanting to get a gun and take a shot at him.'

Mandy shuddered.

'No, the farmers can't stick them. Wombats have got a real bad name for ruining crops and tearing down fences and such like. They're still thought of as pests.'

This was news to Mandy. 'How can they think that? Batty wouldn't harm a fly.'

'That's not the point,' Graham broke in. 'I know what it's like. When we get wombats here at Peppermint Hill, I always know we've got trouble. People want animals that are cute and easy to look after. Old wombats just aren't the flavour of the month, and that's a fact!'

'But Batty's gorgeous!'

'Says you.' Katie stood up and stretched. 'But then, you fall for anything on four legs!'

Mandy had to admit that this was true. She followed Katie back to the Landcruiser, telling

Tim to sit and stay. She turned to Graham. 'You will try to look out for a place for Batty, won't you? Hilda's only got one more week left.'

'I'll ask around,' he promised.

'Me too.' Katie put the car into gear and said goodbye to Graham. 'Don't worry, we'll think of something,' she said to Mandy. 'There's bound to be someone somewhere who's nutty enough to take him on!'

Christmas was coming, and the days grew hotter. Gary's parents, Abbie and Don Simpson, had invited the Hopes over to Waratarah for Christmas Day. They promised them a real Australian celebration. There would be a barbeque by their magnificent pool, and after lunch they would all go down to the beach.

'Bring your swimmies and your boogie board,' Gary told Mandy. He called just after Mandy and Katie got back from Peppermint Hill to collect his bike. They sat together by the side of the creek, dangling their feet in the cool water.

'Hmm.' Mandy wasn't paying attention.

'I said, the Martians have landed in Eurabbie Bay.'

'Oh, great.' She swished her feet in the current.

'And I'm boogie board champion of the world.'

'What? Oh sorry, Gary. I was thinking of something else.'

'It wouldn't be animals, would it?' He laughed. 'I never knew anyone like you. You live on another planet. There are no people, just furry, friendly four-legged creatures!'

'Sorry,' she said again. 'Gary, I don't suppose you want a wombat?' She knew it was a long shot. Abbie and Don Simpson weren't keen to keep pets.

'Yeah, yeah. It's on my Christmas present list,

as a matter of fact.'

'No, I'm serious. They make great pets.'

'You mean it?'

'Hilda Harris has to find a home for Batty.'

'You mean the old lady at Orchard Farm? She's weird.' Gary got up to fetch his bike.

'She's not weird.'

'She is if she keeps pet wombats.'

Mandy stood up to face him.

'They all say she's a weirdo,' he insisted, going red. 'And now I know she is!' He sounded defiant.

She sighed.

'And don't look at me like that!'

'Like what?'

'Staring and not saying anything. You only want to make me feel bad, so I'll agree to take this smelly old wombat back to my place. Why don't *you* do it?'

'We're only here for six months, that's why.' Anyway, her parents had one rule which they always stuck to: Mandy was never allowed to bring any of the animals she rescued back home. Their practice would be overrun by wanderers and orphans if they relaxed that one.

'And I can't either. Wombats dig up flowers

and bushes. My mum would go mad.'

They reached a stalemate.

'But you would like to see him, wouldn't you?' she suggested after a while. 'I'm not saying you should adopt him; I'm just asking if you'd like to take a peek.'

'Well, I *can't* adopt him,' Gary repeated, then paused. 'But I guess it won't do any harm to drop in and take a look.'

She grinned. 'Great. I'll go fetch my bike.'

So they cycled the few kilometres to Orchard Farm, both eager to see the wombat. True, he was tame, and it wasn't like coming across one in the wild, burrowing away at the earth or digging out roots with his sharp front claws, but wombats were getting to be pretty rare. Gary had to admit he was interested. 'How big is he?' he asked, as Hilda's farm came into view.

'About sixty centimetres high and about a metre long. And really fat!'

'Where does she keep him?'

'In the apple loft.'

They whizzed down the hill between the rows of fruit trees. As they drew near to the farm, Mandy sensed a sad emptiness. There were no animals grazing among the apple trees. The chickens had gone from the yard, and even the beehive was silent. They propped their bikes against the fence and stepped up to the door.

Hilda took ages to answer their knock. She smiled weakly when she saw who it was, then invited them in for a drink. The kitchen was full of packing-cases, the shelves and cupboards almost empty. 'You heard the good news about Matilda?' she asked.

Mandy nodded.

'Jim Morris drove down last night in his pick-up truck. That all worked out fine.' Her voice was flat, but she forced another smile. 'If I'm right, I reckon you've come by to sneak another look at old Batty,' she guessed.

Mandy blushed.

'No worries. He'll be glad to see you.' Hilda led them out to the barn and climbed the steps to the loft.

'I mentioned Batty to Graham Masters. I think Merv Pyke is looking out for a good place for him as well,' Mandy told her.

Hilda paused at the door, one hand on the latch. 'Yes, but I don't want him cooped up in a yard in town.' She shook her head. 'He's had it free and easy here at the farm. I let him out in the evening and he goes where he likes. In a way you could say he was half-wild, grubbing around in the dirt. I wouldn't want him to be penned in, see.' She opened the door and stepped into the dark room.

Mandy glanced at Gary. He shrugged. They went in, bending low under the sloping roof, waiting for Batty to come out and say hello. 'He's half-wild.' Hilda's words echoed inside her head.

'Hey, look!' Gary crouched and pointed to the rustling stack of straw in the far corner of the loft. Hilda had coaxed Batty out of his hideaway with a handful of fresh grass roots. Soon his blunt face peered out at them. 'He's just like an old grizzly bear!' he grinned.

'Or a badger.' Mandy held her breath. Slowly Batty plodded towards the treat Hilda held out for him.

'He's cute.'

'Look at his dumpy little legs. And see, he's got no tail at all!'

For a while they watched in fascinated silence.

'Tell you what,' Hilda suggested. 'You wait here while I go and root around for something else he might like to eat. OK?'

Eagerly they nodded.

'He'll sit in the doorway with you if you stay nice and quiet.' Hilda struggled to pick him up from the floor and hand him to Mandy. He was heavy and solid. 'Just hold him gently under his belly like this. That's right. He likes a drop of sunshine, don't you, old mate?' She left them in the warm sun, their backs against the door, Batty snuffling happily on Mandy's lap.

Gary gazed at him. 'Yeah, he's cute.'

'And Hilda isn't weird?'

'I reckon not.' He paused. 'But it's still "no". No way would my mum have a wombat anywhere near the house.'

Mandy sighed. 'I know. But guess what? Something Hilda just said has given me an idea.'

'What's that?' Gary tickled the wombat's nose with a piece of straw. Batty twitched his whole face then coughed.

'She said he's half-wild, remember? She doesn't want him cooped up in a tiny yard.' It turned out that her mum had been right about Hilda not making much effort to find a place for Batty. She really didn't want to see him go to the wrong kind of home.

He nodded. 'So?'

'So, Hilda also said he can dig up his own

roots and stuff. She told me that last time. Maybe that's the answer!'

'Meaning what?'

'Well, maybe I've been on the wrong track, trying to find him a good home and not getting anywhere because people have this idea that wombats wreck your garden and all that.'

'Yeah?'

'Think of it another way. Batty's used to lots of space. Wombats really belong in the great outdoors, don't they?'

'Right!' A look of realisation crept across his face as he began to see what she was getting at.

Mandy stroked Batty's head and gazed out from the loft, across the apple orchard to the hills beyond. 'And if he's half-wild already, why do we need to stick him in a yard in the town somewhere? Why don't we do the opposite? We could do what Graham did with the injured joey yesterday. We could put Batty back into the wild!'

Four

'Why the sudden interest in wombats?' Mandy's dad asked. He came across her taking down the huge book on Australian wildlife from the shelf in the surgery. The page lay open at 'W' for 'Wombat', after 'Wallaby'. 'As if I couldn't guess!' Mandy had rushed home from Orchard Farm full of her great new idea. Now she wanted to learn everything she could about how wombats lived in their natural habitat.

She was too busy to stop for tea, she said. 'Dad, would Batty be a common or a hairy-nosed wombat?' She glanced up, her finger pointing to a place where she'd left off reading. The low sun slanted through the open windows. A cool electric fan whirred overhead.

'Common. The hairy-nosed variety lives further south. Shall I bring you a sandwich?'

She nodded. 'Yes, please. Did you know that wombats in the wild sleep all day in burrows that are sometimes thirty metres long?' Her eyes sparkled as she glanced up to pass on the latest amazing wombat fact. 'They make a sleeping chamber at the end of each burrow and line it with bark.' She paused. This would be the main challenge, she knew; to get lazy old Batty into the habit of digging his own burrow. She wondered what would be the best way to teach him.

'What did Hilda say about releasing him into the wild?' Adam Hope asked quietly. He busied himself by tidying the desk.

Mandy shook her head. 'I haven't told her. Gary said we'd better find out more about it before we said anything. We're going to meet up with Graham at Peppermint Hill after tea. We rang him and he says he can show us a good place to observe some wild wombats, just so Gary and I can get to know how they live. When we've checked everything out, that's when we can ask Hilda what she thinks.'

Mr Hope listened and nodded. 'And what does Graham say?'

Mandy frowned. 'All he said was we didn't have much time to get Batty ready to go back into the bush.' She turned the page and read on. 'Hey, did you know the first sighting of a common wombat was by a convict called James Wilson in 1798. He called it a "whom-batt".'

'And did *you* know, the *last* sighting of a rare Mandy Hope by her family was at midday on the twenty-first of December? They're beginning to think she's become extinct!'

'Sorry, Dad.' She blushed and looked up. 'But this is urgent. You don't mind, do you?'

He smiled. 'No. Your mum and I are worried that you're getting your hopes up too high, that's all. It's not an easy thing to put an animal that's been kept as a pet back into the wild. There are all sorts of hidden pitfalls, and often the animal hasn't learned how to defend itself.'

'I know. That's why we want to go out with Graham and find out all we can first. We will be careful, honestly!'

'Good.' He tilted his head back and rubbed his beard. 'What do you want in that sandwich?'

'Cheese and pickle, please.' Mandy had her nose stuck in the book again. She read that wombats had been overlooked by experts in the past. Koalas and kangaroos were the favourites for study. For some reason, no one found the wombat very interesting. She read on until Gary skidded to a halt on his bike in the yard.

'G'day!' His cheery greeting interrupted her. She closed the book and went out into the warm evening.

'The book says dusk is a good time to see wombats,' she told him as they set off for Peppermint Hill. 'That's when they come out to feed. I think we're going to be lucky.'

'I reckon so,' he said, laid back as ever. As they cycled, he told Mandy about the latest giant wave he'd ridden, giving her a blow-by-blow account of how he'd taken it at the right split second, steered away from the rips that pulled other surfers off course, and gone with the wave until it reached the shore.

Graham Masters took them on foot up a trail that led from the rescue centre across a hillside scattered with eurabbie gum trees. By now the sun had settled low on the horizon. It was a time of long shadows, when spiky echidnas perched on high rocks in what was left of the sun. At ground level the night-loving creatures emerged. Mandy spotted the striped, bushy tail of a bandicoot, and all three of them stopped to watch the amazing mid-air acrobatics of a sugar glider. This flying squirrel floated from tree to tree by spreading its legs wide and unfurling folds of skin that allowed it to glide like a kite across incredible distances. It landed safely, and they went on their way, towards a spot which Graham had pinpointed.

'See, here's a path made by a wombat.' He pointed to a well worn track leading from an open clearing towards a sturdy gum tree. At the end of the track, they found the arched entrance to a deep burrow.

'What's this?' Gary kneeled on one knee and felt with his fingertips round a shallow dish scooped out of the earth at the base of the tree.

'That's his sunbathing spot,' Graham said. 'They sometimes like a lie in the sun.'

'Here's another track!' Mandy followed it to the entrance of another burrow. Soon they'd found at least half a dozen entrances to deep burrows dug into the soft dry earth. 'Are they all made by the same wombat?' she asked.

'No. I've seen quite a few round here.' Graham nodded towards a clump of bushes beside a large boulder. 'That's a good place for us to keep watch from.'

They crept out of sight and settled behind the bushes to wait until the wombats decided to come out for their evening feed.

'They don't bother to cover their tracks, do they?' Mandy whispered. The whole clearing was criss-crossed with their worn-down runs.

'No, but then there's not much to upset these old fellows except fast cars and the odd hungry dingo. Mostly they get left alone.'

Mandy raised her eyebrows. 'That's good!' She was thinking of the dangers Batty might have to face.

'Shh!' Gary warned. 'Look over there!'

They peered through the leaves of their bush as a round, brown head appeared from one of the largest burrows. A pair of short-sighted eyes blinked and took a good look round. Then the wombat crept out of his burrow and trudged along his track. Soon he had his nose to the ground, sniffing out the juiciest blades of sword grass, scratching at them with his sharp front claws and happily munching the tender bases. He moved off slowly through the bush, nose down, snuffling and searching for food.

Then a grunting cough close by distracted them. It came from the burrow nearest to their bush. Another wombat came out to feed, and this time it was followed by a youngster. The baby was already fat and hairy, but only half grown. He stuck close to his mother as they plodded forward into the clearing. Soon mum was choosing the best roots for junior. She dug them up and dropped them on the ground for him to chew.

Mandy's face lit up. She smiled broadly at Graham.

'Watch!' he said. The mother had moved on to start another burrow. She came up the slight hill towards the bush where they were hidden, and began to work right under their noses, scuffing at the earth with her sharp front claws and pushing the loose soil back with her hind feet. Soon her front half had disappeared. All they could see was her squat, tailless backside and the stumpy legs busy scrabbling out earth. Then the whole of her disappeared, leaving the young wombat alone in the clearing.

Then it happened, quick as a flash. There was a streak of yellow at the far side of the clearing, a snarl and a snap of pointed white teeth. The young wombat turned and squealed. The dingo pounced.

Graham was the first to react. He sprang from behind the bush and leaped into the clearing. The dingo glanced away from his prey, strong jaws snapping. It gave the mother time to shoot out of the half-made burrow and dart with surprising speed to defend her helpless baby. She ran full pelt at the dingo, charged and bowled him on to his side with her full weight. He fell off-balance, rolled sideways and saw his intended supper scurry to the safety of the old burrow.

Mandy and Gary followed Graham into the open. Together they managed to herd the dingo away. Though his jaws snapped and his amber eyes flashed angrily, he knew he was beaten. His fine, intelligent head dropped and he turned to slink off into the bush. The last they saw of him was the white flash of the tip of his tail.

By now the female wombat had run, coughing and grunting, after her youngster. The deep burrow was their refuge from danger. The

clearing was empty. The wombats were safe.

But Mandy felt as if she'd been run over. The shock of the dingo's sudden attack had left her drained.

'You OK?' Gary asked.

She nodded.

'That was close.'

'Too close.' She tried not to imagine what would have happened if Graham hadn't jumped up to distract the wild dog. 'I didn't realise wombats could move that fast!'

'Only over short distances,' Graham explained. 'If that dingo had caught them any

further from their burrow, he'd have outrun
them easy. And he'd have had main course and
pudding all in one go!'

Mandy shivered.

'Sorry,' Graham muttered. 'But life is tough
for the old wombat out here in the bush.'

She nodded and sighed. 'You don't think
Batty's up to it, do you?'

'I'd like to see him run that fast,' he admitted.
'Only I don't think he can. He's an old guy,
remember.'

'And would he have spotted the danger?'

'Not if the dingo catches him downwind. He
wouldn't even have a clue that the enemy was
there.'

'The trouble with Batty is he's had a cosy life
so far,' Gary put in. 'He'd never guess there was
a dingo out here waiting to turn him into supper,
even if he did smell him.'

'You reckon?' Graham grimaced and frowned.
He turned to Mandy. 'What about this plan of
yours, then?'

She thought long and hard. 'I don't think he'd
make it out here,' she admitted. 'We don't have
long enough to get him ready for a start. And I
didn't realise there were all these dangers.'

She hated to say it. It was admitting defeat before they'd even tried to train and release him. She turned away and began to walk down the track towards the rescue centre. 'But what do we do?' she whispered to herself. 'If we can't put Batty back into the wild, what on earth's going to happen to him now?'

Five

'Listen, it's not as bad as it looks.' Graham tried to put Mandy's mind at rest as they walked down to the rescue centre.

'But Batty needs someone to look after him!' She knew now that he wouldn't survive long against the likes of the dingo that had just attacked the mother wombat and her baby. And then there were the farmers who came along and blocked up the entrances to their burrows, just because rabbits sometimes took shelter there and the farmers couldn't get at them to destroy them. She'd read about this in her wildlife book.

'Yeah, we're agreed on that.' They'd reached the Peppermint Hill compound. Graham had told them to sling their bikes into the back of the pick-up and to jump into the cab. 'What do you say we take a drive down the track to Hilda's place? I reckon she could use a hand with her packing, and I want to have a chat.'

Mandy and Gary climbed in and sat beside him. The light was fading fast from the hillside as they drove through the groves of nut trees towards Orchard Farm. Meanwhile, Mandy quizzed Graham about what he thought they should do next.

'There's still time to look out for a good home for old Bats,' he assured her. His voice helped her to calm down. He spoke as slow and quiet as ever. No rush. No worries. 'Hang on till I've had a chat with Hilda.'

Mandy relaxed, finding time to listen out for the mad, laughing cry of the kookaburra, and to watch the mobs of kangaroos loping off up the hills. She thought she could spot the joey with the chewed ear. He'd learned his lesson now, it seemed, and stuck close to his mother's side. The small clan hovered by the track, front paws dangling, eyes alert. They were too curious for their own good as they came close to the pick-up and loped alongside.

'Isn't that Merv's van?' Gary pointed to a vehicle in Hilda's yard. The shabby farm had just come into view. Soon they were able to read the red letters on the side of the battered old Land-Rover: 'M. PYKE. EURABBIE GENERAL STORES. FREE DAILY DELIVERIES.' And there was the tall, lean figure of the shopkeeper, slightly stooped, with his grey hair and heavy moustache. He stood, arms folded, deep in conversation with Hilda Harris. Merv's greyhound, Herbie, sat patiently between them.

Merv shook his head as Graham parked the car and the three of them jumped down into the yard. Herbie trotted to greet them, long tail wagging. 'Nah, I've been asking everywhere, but you know how it is, Hilda. It's coming up to Christmas and everyone's got their heads full of how much bread to order for the holidays, and whether or not the world will end if they don't get into Eurabbie to buy their turkey. They don't want to give too much thought to adopting an old wombat.' He sniffed. 'All this stuff about presents and Santa Claus; it beats me!' He frowned at Mandy and Gary, as if Christmas was their fault. 'I reckon it's the silly season. It gets to everyone.' He grumbled on, fixing his brimmed hat firmly on his head.

'But you know I leave for Sydney on Christmas Eve. My nephew, Steve, arrives to collect me and my gear round about midday.' Hilda looked more worried than ever. She gazed towards the barn, and up the steps to the open door of the loft.

'G'day!' Graham shook hands with both Hilda and Merv. Mandy looked on as Herbie suddenly caught sight of Moses slinking out from under the veranda. The greyhound pretended to chase the cat. Moses turned and arched his back. Herbie gave up, lost interest and went to sniff at the base of the steps leading to the apple loft.

'Hey, look at that!' Gary pointed up the steps. They saw Batty's sturdy round shape emerge from the loft to say hello. Herbie's tail wagged to and fro. Graham took the steps two at a time to carry the wombat down. Batty touched noses with Herbie, and they ambled across the yard together.

Mandy laughed. It was like a comedy routine; the thin, smooth, elegant greyhound and the stumpy, shaggy, barrel-shaped wombat. She

watched as Batty set about scrabbling for roots
in the overgrown patch of grass by the fence,
while Herbie sat by. His tail still waved to and
fro in the dust. Then she sighed. 'See, he'd trust
anyone!' Even suspicious old Moses had come
out from the long shadows and sidled up to
Batty to say hello.

Slowly Mandy and Gary tuned into the grown-
ups' conversation.

'I could try Tilly Swann over at Two People
Beach,' Merv suggested. 'She's got a houseful
of animals, all shapes and sizes. Maybe one more
wouldn't make much difference.' He went on
to admit that even he was running out of ideas.

Hilda nodded. 'Good on you.' She glanced at
the trio of animals; cat, dog and wombat, the
only four-footed creatures in sight on the farm
now. She sighed.

Mandy sensed that the old lady had given up.
Something inside her was too sad for words.
She stood, hands in the pockets of her baggy
trousers, gazing into the far distance.

Graham stepped into Merv's place as the
storekeeper glanced up at the vanishing sun,
called Herbie to heel, and prepared to be on
his way. 'Thanks, Merv. Catch you later.' He

turned to Hilda. 'Anyhow, there's always the rescue centre,' he said quietly. 'Batty can come up to Peppermint Hill on Christmas Eve if Merv can't find a place for him.' He smiled kindly.

Mandy nodded. 'That's right. Batty will never be homeless. And we'll visit him, Hilda, so he won't be lonely!'

The old lady pulled herself together. 'Right. Good.' She turned away towards the house.

'Just until everyone gets Christmas out of their systems,' Graham assured her. 'Then in the New Year we can start looking for a place for him again.'

She nodded absent-mindedly. 'Yes, the New Year.'

'So I'll give you a ring on Christmas Eve,' he suggested. 'To see if you need me to call by and collect him.'

'Great.'

Mandy felt puzzled. She looked at Gary. Why wasn't Hilda over the moon about Graham's offer? The rescue centre might not be the final solution to Batty's problem, but there couldn't be anyone better than Graham to look after him in the meantime. Gary shrugged and looked away.

'Wait here a sec. Keep an eye on things,' Graham said to them. He began to follow Hilda into the house.

'That's good, isn't it?' Mandy wandered across the yard with Gary. She bent to stroke Batty's grizzly head. The wombat chewed and grunted. 'You'll be fine up there at Peppermint Hill, won't you, Bats?' She felt relieved that the Christmas Eve deadline had been lengthened. They could safely get over it by taking Batty to Graham's place.

Batty twitched his whiskers and sidled up to her for a closer cuddle. He put his chin on her lap as she crouched down to stroke him.

'I reckon it'll have to do,' Gary agreed.

'It'll be the lap of luxury!' Mandy insisted. 'Like a five star hotel for wombats.' She thought of the clean, orderly rows of kennels and hutches, the wide compounds, the fresh air, good food, and Graham's expert care. 'Why does everyone seem so down about Batty going to Peppermint Hill?'

'No reason. It's OK.' He scuffed his trainer in the dirt.

Thoughtfully Mandy leaned over the fence and pulled at a clump of fresh, sweet-looking grass. She fed it to Batty from the palm of her hand. 'But?' she asked. She could hear a big 'but' in Gary's short, half-hearted replies.

'No, nothing.'

She picked Batty up from the ground and began to walk towards the farmhouse. Graham appeared in the door. There was no sign of Hilda. Mandy persisted. 'There *is* something. I can't work this out. What we're saying is, we know we can't risk letting Batty loose to fend for himself. We know Christmas is a bad time for finding him a new place, especially since Hilda's pretty fussy about where he goes.' Mandy walked with Gary, feeling Batty's solid weight in her arms, enjoying the tickle of his whiskers against her cheek. 'So Graham's idea about putting him up at the rescue centre seems brilliant to me. Only, no one else seems pleased. In fact, I'd say Hilda was nearly in tears. Why, Gary? What's wrong with Peppermint Hill?'

'Nothing. It's probably gonna be OK.' Gary looked at Mandy and saw she wouldn't be fobbed off any longer. 'OK, then. Round here, if an animal's in trouble we take it up to the rescue centre. Graham's terrific. We know the animals get the best treatment. He looks after them, no matter where they come from. Then people can go along and choose a kit or a pup and give them a new home. It's magic, because they go away knowing they've rescued a pup no one else wanted. Everyone's happy. The only thing is, some of the animals don't get lucky.'

'You mean, nobody comes along and chooses them?' She imagined that some older pets might get overlooked. She was sure that most people would go for the sweet kitten with wide eyes, or the playful pup who could be trained from scratch.

Gary nodded. 'Yeah, that happens sometimes.'

'And what if no one comes along and chooses Batty?' She knitted her brows. She began to see that his problems might not be over.

'Well, Graham will hang on to him as long as he can, I reckon.'

'Then what?'

'When the place gets full, there's a problem. There's not a thing he can do about it. The animal that's been there longest gets moved out. That's the way it works.'

She felt her heart miss a beat. 'Moved out? Where to?'

'Well, when I say "moved out", I mean that Graham generally calls in the vet. It's usually Mr Munroe. But now I reckon it'll have to be your mum or dad.' Gary stopped, red in the face, unable to meet her gaze.

'He'd have to be put down!' Mandy said faintly. 'If Batty turned out to be the oldest resident and the rescue centre was full to overflowing, Graham would bring him to Mitchell Gap and we'd have to put him down!'

Gary couldn't bring himself to answer. Mandy's relief turned to dread, as Batty snuggled close, warm and heavy in her arms.

On Christmas Eve Graham phoned Mandy to ask if she wanted to go with him to Orchard Farm to pick up the wombat. It was late morning, and Graham had told her that all Merv's efforts had been in vain. Batty still didn't have a home to go to.

As soon as she came off the phone she went to tell her mum what was happening. 'We're taking Batty to the rescue centre,' she said quietly. 'Is it OK if I go and help?'

Emily Hope stood by the operating table in the surgery. She looked cool and efficient in her clean white coat. She was waiting for an anaesthetic to take effect on her patient, a collie and Labrador cross. Katie was busy laying out dental instruments, while Mrs Hope stood calmly at the dog's head, waiting to take out two painful rotten teeth. She nodded. 'Say goodbye to Hilda from me, and wish her good luck in Sydney.' She checked the dog's jaw reflex to see if he was sound asleep. Then she reached for the forceps.

'You're sure it's OK if I go before surgery's finished?' Mandy was torn between doing her usual jobs here at Mitchell Gap and going over to Hilda's farm.

'Sure I'm sure. It's important.' Her mum looked up and smiled. 'And hey, let's think positively, shall we? You help Graham take the wombat up to his place, then we'll get Christmas over with and hope for the best in the New Year. There's still a good chance of the right person coming along!'

Mandy smiled back. 'Thanks, Mum.'

'And don't let it spoil your Christmas.' She gave her another quick smile and a nod. 'Remember, we've got the barbecue at Waratarah. It'll be our first beach Christmas!'

Mandy knew that the Simpsons' party was something to look forward to. She sped off, pedalling hard on her bike to Peppermint Hill, where she met up with Graham. Then they drove in silence to Hilda's place. It already felt deserted. Petals from blossom trees had fallen to the ground, forming a soft white carpet, drifting into the yard and along the old veranda. Soon Hilda came out to meet them.

'Batty's inside. I've got him safely bedded down in an empty packing-case,' she told them. She was brisk. Her nephew was due any time now. 'I made sure he was nice and cosy. I lined the box with straw and he's got plenty of roots to keep him going.' She led them into the house. 'I'd offer you a drink of juice, but I packed the glasses away somewhere.'

Mandy smiled and shook her head. 'Thanks anyway.'

'Are you all set?' Graham stood in the middle of the kitchen. He looked around for the right packing-case.

'I reckon. Steve's taking me and Moses and just a couple of suitcases. We'll send a truck in the New Year for all the big stuff.' Hilda was wearing a smart navy blue skirt and blouse, totally unlike her usual self.

'Here he is.' Mandy found Batty curled up inside a straw nest in a tea-chest in the corner of the room. Only his round back was visible. He seemed to be able to sleep through it all.

Hilda stayed at the far side of the room. 'We already said our goodbyes,' she murmured. She watched as Graham judged how best to carry the big box into the yard.

'You take that end,' he told Mandy. 'It'll need two of us to lift this. Ready?'

Together they raised the box and carried it

out smoothly to the rescue centre truck. Batty stayed fast asleep.

'Wait here,' he said with a small nod.

Mandy sat in the back of the truck as Graham went back inside the house briefly. She felt her throat begin to hurt with the effort of swallowing a huge lump. She took a deep breath. If she concentrated on the shape of the clouds rolling in from the east, perhaps she could stop thinking about poor Hilda.

Soon Graham came out. He climbed into the cab and started the engine. The open doorway of the old farmhouse gaped dark and empty. At the last moment Mandy saw Hilda appear at the door. The truck turned and rolled out of the yard. She saw the old lady raise her hand and wave. Then she was gone.

The truck rattled up the rough track, raising clouds of dust. Inside his box, deep in the nest of straw, Batty slept on.

Six

Christmas Day in Eurabbie Bay was a lively, colourful affair. Adam Hope, dressed in his brightest pink T-shirt and a pair of swimming-shorts, took charge of the music at Abbie and Don Simpson's poolside party.

'I didn't know your dad was a DJ!' Gary said to Mandy.

'Neither did I.' She felt her toes curl with embarrassment. He was playing golden oldies. This meant that no one under the age of twenty had even heard of the songs he chose. The music was loud, the sun shone bright in a blue sky, and practically everyone except Merv

Pyke ended up in the pool.

Katie was there helping to organise the food, slaving happily behind a sizzling barbecue. Alistair King, the retired vet who sometimes came to lend a hand at Mitchell Gap, was there with his wife, Maggie. He was telling Emily Hope about a holiday they'd taken in the islands off Queensland. She wanted to hear all about the coral of the Great Barrier Reef.

'Too many tourists get up there these days. It's nothing like it was,' Merv cut in with his gloomy remark.

Maggie King laughed. She was used to him putting a dampener on everything. 'Well, Merv, with over a thousand-mile stretch of reef to go at, and millions of tropical fish among the coral, I reckon there's plenty left unspoilt!'

Mandy marvelled at the sheer size of the country. She wondered what fabulous animals lurked in the tropical Queensland rain-forests.

'Can't they turn that din down?' Merv changed the subject but grumbled on.

Emily Hope nodded at Mandy. 'Go and ask your dad to turn the volume down.'

'We can't hear ourselves think.' Merv stuck his face into a pint of beer. When he finished drinking his moustache was covered in white froth.

Mandy ran to the other side of the pool. Her dad strained to hear Merv's request, then fiddled with the controls on the sound system.

'Aah, don't turn it down!' Suzi Peratinos pleaded. 'We can hardly hear it!' She was doing a wild dance with shy Mal Stalker. Other kids from the beach had come up to Waratarah to join in the fun.

By late afternoon the party was in full swing. Mandy's dad, by now disguised as Santa Claus, insisted on playing Christmas carols full-blast. Her thoughts turned to Batty. Not that she'd completely forgotten him. Through the excitement of opening presents that morning, through the chatting and dancing of the party, he was there at the back of her mind. She'd loved every minute of her day, including the surfing session at midday. But now she felt Christmas wouldn't be complete without a visit to the rescue centre to see how Batty was settling in. So she borrowed Gary's bike and left them to it, setting off for Peppermint Hill with a small present for Graham. His Christmas Day would be pretty much like any other; the animals still had to be fed and looked after.

She found him hard at work hosing down the kennel yard. He waved as he spotted her riding in through the gate.

'Hi, how's Batty?' Mandy jumped off the bike and ran through the gate in the tall wire fence into the kennel yard. She thrust the brightly wrapped gift at him. 'Mum and Dad say Happy Christmas!'

'Thanks. He's good. No worries.' Graham led her to the end of the row of kennels. 'I put him in here. He's got a big hutch at the back, with plenty of sleeping space, and an area at the front where he can sit in the sun and feed.'

They walked down the row to the excited yapping of dogs of all shapes and sizes. There was a dalmatian with a deep bark and fine black and white markings, a pretty cream poodle, a scruffy terrier crossbreed, and many more. Their din was deafening as they passed by. Mandy's soft heart melted. If she could, she would have taken every single one home there and then.

When they reached the last kennel in the row, there was no sign of the wombat. 'Come on in,' Graham said. He opened the inner door,

picking up a handful of roots from a heap in
the corner.

Mandy watched as he bent to peer into the
large hutch. She could hear old Batty scuffling
around inside. Soon he poked his head out of
the arched entrance to the wooden hutch, his
whiskers and nose twitching at the smell of food.

'Hi, Bats!' Mandy forced a cheerful note into
her voice. It was like visiting a sick relative in
hospital. The rescue centre, though good, was
nothing like Orchard Farm, where Batty had had
the free run of the apple loft and could scratch
in the yard to his heart's content.

'Not exactly home from home, eh?' Graham
read her thoughts. 'It never is. Don't worry, we'll
work hard to get him out of here as soon as we
can.'

'No, it's very good,' Mandy insisted. It was all
beautifully clean and well looked after. Graham
cared for his animals, giving them good food
and plenty of exercise. Often they were in a far
better condition when they went out of the
rescue centre than when they'd come in. 'Batty's
lucky you could find room for him.'

'Well, I'll make sure Bats stays fit and healthy,'
he assured her. He handed the roots to Batty,

who nibbled and picked at first, then soon began chomping heartily.

Mandy crouched to watch him. 'Do you think he'll pine for Hilda and Orchard Farm?'

Graham stood behind her, hands on hips. 'I can't say. But I reckon so, after how long?'

'Thirteen years.'

He whistled. 'At any rate, he's not gone off his tucker!'

'No way!' Mandy smiled as the wombat munched his way through a healthy salad of grass, roots and fungi piled into his feeding dish.

'And do you reckon someone will come along to adopt him?' It was the question that preyed continually on her mind.

'Can't say that for sure either. I *have* seen people fall for a wombat before, especially a young one. Mal Stalker's family got Harry from Peppermint Hill, but that was before my time. I hear Harry's mother got shot and he was an orphan when they brought him in here. Had to be hand-reared.'

Mandy was shocked. 'Who shot the mother?'

'A farmer, I reckon.' Graham shrugged.

'They can't do that now, can they?'

'No, they made a law. That doesn't mean

to say wombats are the farmers' best mates, though.' He folded his arms across his chest.

Mandy scratched Batty's head, happy to see him adapting well to his new home. The yelping from the kennels had died down, and the place felt warm and friendly. 'Did Hilda get off OK yesterday?' She stood and followed Graham back into the open yard.

'According to Merv, she did. Funny thing that; there she is in Sydney, and the old place is locked up for good.' Graham shook his head. 'Thanks for the present.' He tapped the parcel which he'd tucked into his shirt pocket.

She grinned. 'Thanks for looking after Batty.'

'No worries.'

She nodded and picked up her bike. 'I'll pop in and see him every now and then, if you don't mind. I want to keep in touch with Hilda and tell her he's OK.'

'Good, I reckon she'd like that.'

Mandy smiled back. 'Happy Christmas, Graham.' She launched off up the track, back to Waratarah and the Simpsons' party.

'Yeah, Happy Christmas!' He waved, to a background chorus of barks, miaows, grunts, coughs and brays. Batty of course stayed silent, his mouth full, his mind fixed on the important business of eating.

Over the New Year both Gary and Mandy became regular visitors at Peppermint Hill. During the week after Christmas, they saw the dalmatian go to a good home in town, and the pretty poodle to a lonely widow in Mitchell. Day by day the kennels emptied and filled up again, but nobody stopped by Batty's cage to say, 'He's cute; let's take *him*!' Instead, the wombat wore a lonely track inside his earth compound, up and down, up and down the length of the wire fence, gazing out at the wild hillside, scratching at the dry dirt.

It was the end of January. Mandy was beginning to fret badly over Batty. One warm evening, as she and Gary parted at the gate of the rescue centre, she put her fears into words. 'You know this place is full to bursting?' she said quietly. 'Graham just brought in three puppies. Someone found them abandoned in a shed up at Mitchell. He says he can't think where to put them.' Her blue eyes wrinkled into a frown.

'No worries. People will come and snap them up before you know it.' He tried to sound confident. Then he stopped to think ahead. 'You mean, there isn't any space at all?'

She shook her head. 'And Batty's no nearer to finding a home.'

'It's like Death Row in there,' Gary muttered, his happy-go-lucky shell starting to crack.

'Graham says it's got a lot to do with people giving pets as presents at Christmas. That's why the rescue centre's getting crowded out now.'

People never got the message that an animal was for life. They still went on giving them away for Christmas, and their owners brought them to places like Peppermint Hill and the SPCA as soon as the newness of the gift wore off. Mandy felt angry with the owners, but most of all sorry for the unwanted pets. It meant that old, long-stay residents at the rescue centre, like Batty, got pushed further and further down the line.

'Are the pups OK?'

'I think so. You should see them. They're cute!' She smiled briefly. 'Black and white mongrels, a real mixture.' Then she sighed. 'Cute!' That's just it. That's what old Bats isn't, according to most people.'

'*I* like him!' Gary said stoutly.

Mandy felt helpless. 'Me too.' She sighed

again. Tonight she planned to write to Hilda to tell her how Batty was. 'See you at school tomorrow?'

He nodded and said goodbye, then they pedalled off in opposite directions. Before long, Mandy caught sight of Merv's old Land-Rover. It had stopped in a dip in the middle of the road, not far ahead. She frowned. It was late in the day for Merv to be making deliveries. She slowed down, wondering what he could be up to.

Drawing level with the car, she found the driver's door open, but no sign of the crochety shopkeeper. This was odd. The road was single track, too narrow for another car to pass. 'Merv?' She dismounted and let her bike fall against the grass verge. 'Merv, where are you?'

There was no answer. Mandy climbed into the van and peered into the back. Its shelves were almost bare, though the smell of fresh bread still lingered. 'Merv? Herbie?'

Again, no reply. She jumped back on to the road. Over the fence, in a field of ripening corn, she saw a flattened track where someone had recently walked. She decided to follow it. This was too peculiar to ignore. Where were Merv and his dog? And why had he abandoned his car?

The track cut across the corner of the cornfield towards a shaded area of trees and shrub. Mandy hesitated at the edge of the woods. The shadows grew dark and deep. She didn't fancy exploring alone much further.

'Merv?' She called again, louder this time, knowing that the trees would muffle her voice.

'Here!' a gruff voice called back. 'Stay there, I'm on my way!'

She heard a rustling in the bushes to the right. Twigs cracked underfoot. Soon a tall figure emerged. It was Merv, carrying something wrapped up inside his light zip-up jacket; an object which Mandy couldn't yet make out.

Relieved, she swung one leg over the fence to set foot in the shadows of the trees. Merv had shown up in one piece, coming towards her in his shirt-sleeves, his face set in firm lines. 'What have you got there?' she asked. He seemed to be carrying the bundle with great care. She spotted Herbie trotting at his heels, tail down, subdued.

'Stand back!' Merv ignored her and climbed the fence from the other side. There were twigs and leaves in his grey hair. There was a long scratch down his cheek, made by brambles or a sharp branch. 'Look what I spotted by the roadside!' He was breathing hard, and sounded angry as he unfolded one corner of his jacket.

Inside, Mandy glimpsed what looked like a bundle of skin and bones. 'What is it?' she gasped.

'Dog. German shepherd. Half-starved.' His reply came short and jerky. 'Saw it in my wing mirror; thought it was a dingo at first. Have you ever seen anything like it?'

The dog shivered inside his cover, in spite of the warm evening. It badly needed both food and water. 'Do you know who it belongs to?' Mandy asked.

Merv shook his head. 'She's not from round here. No collar. Nothing. When I saw what a state she was in, I pulled up to help. I reckon she thought I was up to no good, so she tried to head off into the wood. Poor thing, she could hardly drag herself along.'

Mandy reached out to stroke the dog's head. She whimpered and tried to lick her hand. 'What will you do now?'

'Take her up to Peppermint Hill.' Merv turned

and ordered Herbie into the van. The greyhound jumped obediently on to the front seat. Merv looked at Mandy. 'Will you sit with her while I drive?'

She nodded and climbed in without a second thought. She settled the stray dog's head on her lap. Then it struck her: the rescue centre was full. Not just nearly full, with one or two kennels to spare, but full to bursting. Graham was already trying to find space for the three orphaned pups. One more rescued animal would be one too many. 'Why don't we take her to my place at Mitchell Gap?' she gabbled. 'My mum and dad would be able to help!' The poor dog whimpered and trembled inside her cover.

Merv shook his head. 'The rescue centre's closer. It's just up the hill. That's the place for this one.' He put the van into gear.

'But she might need treatment!'

'No, just food and water. Graham knows what to do.'

Mandy bit her lip.

Merv shot her a look as they eased forward. 'What's the problem? Look, she's a stray, isn't she? Who'd pay the vet's bill if we took her to your place? I'm not made of money, am I?' He was determined to head for Peppermint Hill.

And Mandy couldn't argue. She knew he was right. The dog desperately needed shelter and the good treatment that Graham could offer.

She sat in silence as the van struggled up the hill. Soon the rescue centre came in sight. She looked at the sign over the gate, spoke soothingly to the suffering animal. 'There, there, girl, you'll soon be OK!'

They saw Graham come out of his living quarters as he heard the van draw up. Merv leaned out of his window and yelled the news. 'Stray dog! Starving to death! Can you do something for her?' He leaped out and came to open the door on Mandy's side.

Graham clicked into action as she handed the stray down to him. 'Open up the kennel gate, Merv! Quick as you can! Good, now let's get her seen to!'

The two men worked urgently to care for the dog, but Mandy sat as if stunned. She was glad that Merv had saved her life. No one, nothing, should suffer like this poor abandoned creature. But his good deed was terrible news for Batty.

After what seemed like an age, Graham came out of the kennels towards the van.

'How is she?' Mandy whispered.

Graham rested his arm against the open door. 'She's gonna be fine.'

'Good.'

He sighed and looked anxiously at her. 'You know I'm gonna have to ring Mitchell Gap about old Bats?'

'Yes.'

'What can I do?' he pleaded.

'No, nothing.' Her voice was drained, her head sank forward.

'OK, well Merv says he'll drive you home. I'll ring your folks after breakfast tomorrow.' Graham took a step back and closed the door as Merv climbed into the driver's seat.

Mandy stared straight ahead, her eyes blurred with tears. She couldn't bear to look at the kennels. Poor Batty's time was up, and there wasn't a thing she could do about it.

Seven

That night, Mandy put off writing her letter to Hilda in Sydney. The dreaded phone call from Peppermint Hill came early next morning, but Graham's news was the last thing anyone could have expected.

Adam Hope answered the phone. Mandy sat in reception nearby, praying that it wouldn't be Graham.

'Yes. Hi, Graham.' Her dad stood, ready for the bad news. 'Mandy tells us you've got a problem. You need to talk to me about Hilda Harris's wombat?'

Mandy sat through what seemed like a long

pause. There was a death sentence hanging over Batty's head. She wished that time would stop, that something, anything would happen to save him.

'What's that?' Her dad sounded surprised. 'He never has! Well, the old rascal!' He shook his head, dumbfounded. 'This morning? It must've been pretty early. It's empty? No, that's right, you won't need us any more. Yes, I'll tell Mandy. Thanks.' He put down the phone.

Mandy slid down from her stool and came slowly towards him. Something unexpected had happened. 'What's wrong?'

'Huh!' He scratched his head. 'Would you believe it? The old wombat's done a runner!'

'What do you mean?' Her heart raced.

'Well, Graham went to check him first thing this morning and he found the kennel empty! No wombat. He says he looked everywhere. He found some damage to the wire fence, and all the earth underneath was scooped away. It looks like Batty took it into his head to dig his way to freedom!'

Mandy gasped. 'He escaped!' As if he knew his time at the rescue centre had run out, he'd taken matters into his own hands. Now her dad wouldn't have to drive over there. Batty had solved the problem of overcrowding for them!

'Hang on, it's not all good news.' Mr Hope wanted to keep her feet on the ground. 'We have to keep our fingers crossed that he can look after himself in the wild.' He waited to let this sink in. 'Of course, there's nothing we can do about that now.'

Mandy took a deep breath. 'Still, at least he's got a chance, that's the main thing!' She said she would like to whizz over to Peppermint Hill before she went on down to school. She wanted to see for herself the tunnel that Batty had dug in his bid for freedom.

She set off, half-relieved, half-worried. She told herself that if Batty was clever enough to do what he'd just done, then surely he had a good chance of surviving on his own. He'd proved he could dig, at any rate!

Graham welcomed her and quickly led her to the end kennel. Sure enough, a hole had been dug big enough for the wombat to wriggle under the fence. 'It looks like he had a go at the wire before he decided that the best way out was to dig,' Graham told her. 'I couldn't believe my eyes when I first saw it. I never thought Bats had it in him!'

On the way out, he took her to see the rescued
German shepherd. She recognised Mandy and
wagged her tail, still too weak to stand. Mandy
stroked her gently. How could anyone let her
get into such a state? 'She's so thin!'

'She'll soon put on weight. Merv says she's
most likely a stray. He found her in the nick of
time!'

Mandy felt glad. She knew the dog was in very
good hands. 'Will you put her in Batty's kennel
when she's well enough?'

Graham nodded.

'Do you think Batty knew?'

'You can never tell. Maybe he knew *something*
was up. I dunno.' Graham wouldn't commit
himself.

But Mandy was convinced that animals knew
what they needed to do to survive. She came
out into the yard with Graham. Together they
gazed up the hillside, into the wild scrub where
Batty had vanished. 'I don't suppose you tried
to look for him?'

Graham shrugged. 'What was the point? I'd
rather Bats took his chances out there, wouldn't
you?'

Slowly she nodded. 'But I can't help

wondering how he's getting on.' She picked up her bike, ready to cycle on to school.

'I reckon we'll never know.' Graham gave a smile and a wave. 'Let's say, we just have to keep our fingers crossed!'

That morning, Mandy couldn't wait to get to school. She free-wheeled down the final hill into Eurabbie, longing to find Gary and tell him the latest news.

He was waiting for her at the main gate, surrounded by gangs of kids in bright T-shirts and jeans, all chatting and making their way towards the modern, two-storey building that was Eurabbie Bay Intermediate School.

She got off her bike and half ran towards him. 'Batty isn't going to be put down!' The words tumbled out. 'Isn't that great? Well, it's not completely great. I mean, he didn't find a good home or anything. It's not that. But he decided to escape! That's what I'm trying to say. Batty dug his way out of the rescue centre!'

Gary stared at her. 'When was that?'

'Some time last night.' She drew breath as they walked together towards the bike shed. 'I'm so pleased. I was dreading my dad having to bring him to Mitchell Gap. That would have been terrible!'

'Yeah.' He walked, one hand pushing his bike, one hand in his pocket, hardly reacting at all. It seemed like he had something else on his mind. 'Does anyone know what happened to him?'

'No, it looks like he just wandered off.' This was the less positive bit. 'I know we didn't want to put him back in the wild, but he did decide to do this himself.' They heard the school bell ring for registration, locked up their bikes and hurried into the main building, down clean light corridors to their crowded classroom.

'Are you glad he's gone?' Gary asked.

'Yes and no. I'll miss him. And I'll be worried sick, wondering how he's coping.' She realised that Gary definitely had something on his mind. He was only half listening and seemed to have gone red under his deep tan. He fiddled with the fasteners on his schoolbag. 'How about you?'

'Yeah,' he agreed.

The teacher, Mrs Bertram, came into the room. Gradually the noise eased. She got out the register and began calling out names.

'Is something wrong?' Mandy whispered. She

tried to catch his eye before they split up for different lessons.

'No.' He took a deep breath and puffed out his cheeks. Then he slung his bag over his shoulder. Mrs Bertram had closed the register and was reading out notices. 'Well, yeah, actually. Meet me after school?'

Puzzled, Mandy nodded. 'Fine. Where?'

'At the bike shed. I have to show you something.'

And that was it. She had to control her curiosity all through Home Economics, Maths, English and Biology. Somehow she grew convinced that this had something to do with Batty. Gary hadn't shown much surprise when she met him with news of the wombat's great escape, and she wasn't sure how he felt about it. Yet, over the weeks he'd grown close to Batty. The school day dragged by. Even Biology didn't hold her attention; her mind was on Gary, and what it was that he wanted to show her.

The bell for the end of school rang at last, and hundreds of students poured out of the building. Some headed towards town, some straight to the beach. Mandy went to meet Gary. She found him by the bike shed trying to put off Dean and the gang who wanted him to go boogie boarding with them.

'Hi.' He stood uncertainly astride his bike. 'Ready?'

'Sure. Where are we going?' She followed him across the yard, out of the gate and up the hill out of town.

'Your place.' He pedalled silently.

'We are? What for?' She had to work hard to keep up with him as the hill grew steeper.

At first Gary wouldn't answer. 'I'll tell you when we get there . . . if he's still there!'

'Who? What are you talking about?' This time Gary had taken his habit of doing plenty but not saying much too far. 'Is this something to do with Batty?' She managed to overtake him on a downhill stretch, as her house came into view. 'Is there something you're not telling me?' She braked and swung round to confront him. She made him pull up before they finally reached Mitchell Gap.

They'd stopped by the creek that ran down by the side of the house, near a big old acacia tree that overhung the clear running water.

'I said I'd show you,' he insisted. He dropped

his bike by the roadside and cut across to the far side of the creek, jumping nimbly from stone to stone.

Mandy followed. They skirted behind the house and surgery, then climbed towards an old disused farm trailer, overgrown with weeds and grass. It must once have belonged to a neighbouring farmer, but had long since been abandoned at the edge of the surgery land.

Gary slowed down and warned Mandy to stay quiet. Carefully he hoisted himself on to one of the large deflated tyres. He peered into the high-sided truck and nodded. 'It's OK; he's still here!' He edged along, to let Mandy climb up beside him. She stared into the trailer. Someone had dropped in armfuls of dry grass and a small pile of roots. The same someone had made it into a safe hiding-place for a fairly large animal. Mandy noticed the stack of grass shift and rustle. Out came the blunt nose and large friendly head of a wombat. There was no mistaking him. 'Batty!' she cried.

Gary nodded. 'Right first time.'

'But how? How did he get here?' She clung to the side of the trailer. 'He couldn't climb in by himself, could he?'

'No. I put him in.'

'When?' There she'd been, picturing Batty in the wild, fending for himself, when all the time he was tucked away safe not two hundred metres from her own house.

'This morning. There was no one around.'

Mandy glanced down the hill towards the low white house. 'Does anyone else know you've put him here?'

Gary shook his head. 'I meant to come down and tell you. But I chickened out.'

'Shh. Let's climb in with him. It's OK, Batty. It's OK, boy; it's only us.'

The wombat scuffled and retreated into the heap of hay, trying hard to hide his bulky shape. Soon all three of them were safely hidden by the high sides of the trailer. Mandy put an arm round Batty's chunky neck. It felt like they were stowaways on a ship. 'Shh!' she whispered. The wombat grunted and coughed. Mandy wanted to hear the full story from Gary. 'What happened?' She turned to him, her eyes shining.

'Well . . .' He cleared his throat. 'Last night I didn't get to sleep for ages. I was thinking about old Bats and what was going to happen to him.'

'Me too.'

'And I woke up early. I don't know why I did it, but I got up before it was light. I wanted to shoot over to Peppermint Hill before it was too late.'

'To say goodbye?'

He nodded.

Mandy knew that this took some nerve. 'I couldn't face doing that,' she confessed. Batty scuffled and grunted. 'Shh!' she warned.

'I left a note for my folks, saying I'd gone down the beach early. But I went right on over to the rescue centre. By this time it was getting light.'

'And what happened? Did you find Batty

wandering up the hill to meet you?' She thought that the cunning old thing had already dug himself free. 'That was lucky!'

'Hmm.' He bit his lip. 'Not exactly.' There was another pause.

'Gary, are you saying that when you got there he was still in his kennel?'

'Sort of. Look, I had to creep up real quiet so as not to set the dogs off barking. Batty's kennel was right at the end of the row, you know? So I crept up.' Gary began to mime the actions, reliving the moment. 'I found him wide awake. He was about the only thing around that was, apart from the roos further up the hill.'

'And what was he doing?'

'Digging.'

'How far had he got?'

'He was about halfway under the fence, digging like crazy. Earth was flying up everywhere, his front claws were going like mad and he was shovelling the earth out with his back legs.'

'And?'

'I just thought I'd better give him a hand to speed things up a bit.' Gary shrugged, sitting hunched up in the old trailer. He had blades of dry grass in his hair and on his T-shirt. 'That's about it.'

She gazed at him. 'You helped him to escape!'

'I reckon.'

Her face broadened into a grin. 'How did you do it?'

'I kind of held the fence up while he dug. He got out twice as fast.'

'Then what?'

'Well, he was out of the tunnel, under the fence, looking pleased with himself, wondering what to do next. But he decided the big wide world was a pretty scary place. I was hissing "shoo!" and waving my arms about, but he just sat there. I got down on my knees and told him to scram, but he nuzzled up to me and sat right down on my foot. No way was this old wombat gonna move!'

By now Mandy was smiling from ear to ear. She scratched Batty's broad bald snout.

'I couldn't leave him, could I? What was I meant to do?' Gary spread his hands in appeal. 'So I picked him up and carried him. I could see Graham's shutters opening, and there were other signs of life. A couple of dogs started to bark. I reckoned we'd best make a quick getaway.' He glanced straight at Mandy's face. 'He weighs a ton!'

'I know he does,' she agreed. 'So why bring him to my place?'

'I reckoned you'd know what to do. But by the time I got here, everyone was already up, having breakfast. Your dad was doing his early morning swim. I couldn't walk up to the house and ask for you, not with old Bats stuck under my arm. I spotted this trailer just up the hill. I reckoned no one was gonna find him if I stuck him in here for the day. I wasn't sure, mind.'

'Is that why you didn't say anything at school?'

'Yeah, sorry. But what if your mum or dad, or Katie or someone had spotted him? I'd get your hopes up, and then we'd get back and find they'd had to put him down after all.'

She nodded, suddenly serious. 'It's OK.' She stopped to think. 'I'm really glad you did what you did. The great escape!'

Gary blushed. 'So what now?'

They gazed down at Batty, who decided to pull himself up on to his short legs, stretch and amble towards the supply of roots. He seemed happy just munching away, turning towards them with what looked like a smile.

'Batty, you're hopeless!' Mandy sighed. 'You had your big chance this morning, and you blew it!' With Gary's help he'd got under the fence and had a tiny taste of freedom.

'It looks like the wild's not where he wants to be,' Gary pointed out.

'Hmm.' Mandy leaned forward and eased herself out full length along the boards of the trailer. She propped herself on her elbows, eye to eye with Batty. 'Wombat!' she said slowly, pointing at him and tickling his chin. Then she waved her hand over the top of the truck. 'Wild. That's where you belong. Understand? Wombat in the wild!'

But Batty came up and nuzzled her face. How long could they keep him hidden here? What would Graham or her mum and dad do if they found out what had happened? Didn't this old wombat realise he was living on borrowed time?

'I reckon he doesn't want to know,' Gary put in. Batty wandered up to him and nestled close to his side.

Mandy rolled over on to her back, then sat up. She narrowed her eyes and fixed them on the lazy pet. 'And *I* reckon he'll just have to learn!'

'What? Are we gonna train him?'

'We're going to show him how to dig a burrow and build a nest, find food, defend himself from dingoes. And this time we really mean it. We'll train Batty to go back where he belongs if it's the last thing we do!'

Eight

Mandy's determination showed on her face as she and Gary went down the hill and into the house for a cold drink. They'd left Batty carefully hidden in the old farm trailer. It was teatime, and both her mum and her dad were taking it easy on the veranda.

'Uh-oh!' Adam Hope nudged his wife's arm. 'Why do I get the funny feeling that Mandy's a girl with a mission?' He studied the slight frown, the concentration written in the straight line of his daughter's mouth and the set of her jaw.

'Don't tease,' Emily Hope murmured. She lay

back on the sun-lounger, eyes half-closed.

Mandy gave them a half-hearted 'Hi!'. Then she and Gary went into the cool kitchen. She took orange juice from the fridge and poured it into two glasses. 'The thing is,' she confided in a whisper, 'if we plan to get Batty into shape, ready to look after himself, we'll have to do it late at night and early in the morning. That's when wombats dig their burrows and find their food.'

Gary nodded. 'You mean, how can we do that without letting on to your mum and dad?'

'I don't think we can.' Mandy couldn't see how her mum and dad would fail to notice. This was going to take quite a few days, maybe even weeks. It would mean giving up a lot of time. How could Gary come over to Mitchell Gap at dawn each morning to help train Batty, and at the same time make it look as if he was just dropping in for a friendly chat? 'No, it wouldn't work,' she decided. 'I guess I could just about keep it secret if it was only me, but you're the one who actually saved Batty's life, and it wouldn't feel right if I went ahead by myself.'

Gary smiled. 'Thanks, Mandy. So you reckon we'll have to tell them where the old boy is?'

She knew in her heart that this was what she wanted to do. 'Well, they already suspect something is up. And I'd feel better if we did.' After all, there was a big difference between bringing a pet back to Mitchell Gap, which she knew wasn't allowed, and trying to put an animal back into the wild. 'I don't think they'll mind,' she said.

He looked relieved.

They drank their juice and stood up from the table. 'Let's tell them now!' She couldn't help feeling nervous as they went out on to the veranda.

'Uh-oh, she's shuffling her feet!' Adam Hope looked round. There was a smile lurking behind his beard and a twinkle in his brown eyes.

Her mum sat up. 'OK, spit it out, you two.' She tried to keep her own mouth straight.

Mandy cleared her throat.

'Father, I cannot tell a lie!' her dad quipped. 'Isn't that the famous saying? Anyway, I feel a confession coming on!'

His jokey tone helped break down her nervousness.

'Honestly, Dad, I'm trying to be serious. We've got something important to tell you.'

'Go ahead,' Mrs Hope said gently. 'Take no notice of your father. What is it?'

'It's Batty.' She glanced at Gary and saw that he too now had his fingers firmly crossed.

'The vanishing wombat!' Adam Hope gave his wife a shrewd look.

'Yes, well, he didn't exactly vanish.'

'No? I thought Graham said he high-tailed it off into the bush? Except wombats don't have tails, do they?'

'Dad! Actually, he didn't make it as far as the bush.'

'Really!' Adam Hope looked surprised. 'You don't mean to say . . . ?'

'No, I don't. Listen, Mum, what I'm trying to tell you is, Gary was out there at the rescue centre this morning, and he . . . well . . . he kind of helped Batty to escape.' Now she'd said it, she felt she had to rush on. 'Only *helped*, mind you. Batty would have got out of the kennels in any case. But when Gary gave him a hand and tried to shoo him off up the hillside, he refused to go! So Gary had to pick him up, and he headed over here with him because he couldn't think what else to do, and . . .' She slowed down. ' . . . Well, actually, Gary hid him in the old trailer at the back of the creek. That's where he is now!'

Her dad's mouth dropped open. 'There's a turn-up for the books!'

Her mum laughed. 'Is Batty OK?' she asked.

Mandy nodded. 'He's fine. And we've got a plan to help him. Do you want to hear it?'

'Please.' Emily Hope got up and strolled along the veranda. She shaded her eyes with one hand and gazed up the hill towards the creek.

'We want to train Batty to take care of himself so that he can go free.'

There was a doubtful silence. Her mum turned to her. 'Didn't you have the same idea before Hilda left Orchard Farm?'

'Yes, but there wasn't enough time. We realised we couldn't just shove him out there to defend himself against dingoes and everything. But this time we can do it nice and slowly. We don't mind how long it takes. Eventually Batty's bound to get the right idea, and then we can let him go without any worries. Gary wants to help!' Her eyes were wide, she held her breath. She needed both her mum and her dad to agree to this.

Mrs Hope glanced back at the rickety trailer

on the hill, just visible in the long grass. She looked at her husband. 'It's a tricky business, putting an animal back into the wild. How would you go about it?' she asked.

Gary spoke for the first time. 'I reckon we could camp out at night and keep an eye on him. I'd let down the ramp at the back of the trailer so he could come and go. We'd be right there, making sure he didn't get into trouble.'

Mandy nodded. 'And we'd show him how to make a burrow, nice and close to the house. In fact, there's a spot by that old acacia tree where there's lots of loose soil by the roots. That would be a good place, wouldn't it?'

'I see.' Her dad considered this quietly. 'You'd give him a start, then he'd get the idea and go on digging a deeper burrow for himself. Is that right?'

They both nodded.

'It's a lot of work, but it sounds possible!'

Mandy gave a little jump into the air. 'Does that mean we can go ahead?' She turned to her mum.

Emily Hope smiled and shook her head. 'What else can you do to help Batty?' She thought long and hard. 'Yes, why not? It's a good job it's the weekend; you can get started right away. Fetch the tents out of the pool storeroom, get yourselves organised. Gary, you'd better check this with your parents, say you need to stay over. The sooner old Bats learns how to use his freedom, the better!'

Everyone agreed that there was no other solution to the problem.

Then it was all action. Mandy ran to find the tents stored in the pool room and Gary phoned home. As soon as he got the go-ahead from his parents, he rushed up the hill to help Mandy pitch the tents. He found her leaning over the side of the trailer.

'It's for your own good!' she explained to the wombat in a stern voice. 'We'll show you how. We want to be able to write to Hilda in Sydney and tell her how fantastic you are! How you've learned to do everything for yourself at your age!' She paused. 'If Hilda can learn to live a new kind of life, so can you!'

Gary let her run on, then he coughed. She spun round to see him standing there. 'So, we're talking to wombats now!' He grinned. 'Don't worry, I won't tell anyone you've gone nuts!'

She jumped down, grabbed a handful of grass and threw it at him. The blades scattered over his head. 'You're as bad as I am, Gary Simpson, and you can't deny it!'

'OK, OK!' He put up his arms in surrender. 'I admit it. I already gave Bats a good talking to earlier this morning! Now, let's get these tents up and give him his first lesson in outdoor pursuits. Come on, let's get moving, it'll be dark before we know it!'

Mandy lifted Batty out of the trailer to let him see what was going on. Together she and Gary worked to pitch the tents before dusk fell. Lazy Bats looked on, curious but puzzled. Soon he turned his attention to some nearby juicy grass roots, little suspecting that his real education for life was about to begin.

'No, Batty, not like that!' Mandy whispered. He was kicking earth back into the burrow they'd started to dig. It was almost dark. Several heaps of soil lay piled where they'd tried in vain to get him to make a home for himself. 'You have to kick it this way, *out* of the hole!' She went down on all fours to show him how. Bats was maddeningly slow to catch on. She shot an

exasperated glance at Gary.

He held the torch steadily on the roots of the acacia tree. 'Do you want me to have a go?'

Wearily she stood up. 'Yes, please. At least he digs his own roots!' Batty was working hard at tearing out and grasping the grass stems and munching slowly through them. Mandy saw this as a mini-triumph.

Gary handed her the torch and took up the task of scrabbling at the loose earth. 'Can you hand me a couple of pieces of bark?'

Mandy swung the torch towards a carefully collected pile of dry bark and thin strips of wood. She'd read in her book that this was what wombats used to line their burrows. Taking a couple of good, flat pieces, she showed them to Batty, who sniffed them. Then she handed them on to Gary to work with. 'See, Bats, this is what you do!' she encouraged.

Batty sat down, his broad head cocked to one side.

By now Gary had half disappeared down the tunnel they'd made. He lined the bottom with the bark, then reversed out. Mandy shone the torch on him; his face was smudged with dirt, his fair hair scattered with bits of loose bark. 'Try putting him in now,' he suggested.

Gently, speaking softly to him, Mandy picked Batty up and carried him to the man-made burrow. She put him inside the entrance. He sniffed and took a waddling step forward. Mandy and Gary held their breaths.

Batty sneezed, sighed and came back out, chugging like a little steam-engine. He blew out his fat cheeks at them, blinked once and turned to head for the trailer. He stumped up the ramp which Gary had managed to lower. Up he went, into the comfort and safety of his pile of straw. Home sweet home!

* * *

This was the first night of Batty's training programme. Mandy and Gary marked it down as a complete failure. The wombat snored the night away in the trailer. Perhaps the straw reminded him of his apple loft at Orchard Farm.

Mandy suggested that they try lining one of their purpose built burrows with straw instead of tree bark. They tried this first thing next morning. No good; Batty expertly dug his own breakfast from the bank by the stream, but when they showed him his luxury, straw-lined burrow, he turned tail and trudged up into the trailer to sleep the day away.

That evening they tried again. Persistence would pay off, Mandy's dad told them, when he came up the hill with a tray of warm cocoa and biscuits for their supper.

Not interested! Batty's actions indicated. He shunned their shelter once more.

They spent Saturday night in their own tents, with hardly a wink of sleep. Adam Hope had advised them to leave the ramp of the trailer down, so that the wombat could come and go as he pleased. When Mandy crawled out of her tent on Sunday morning, she prayed that Batty would still be close by. It was too soon for him to go walkabout. To start with, he needed to learn to dig a burrow; first things first. She searched the trailer, found it empty, and woke Gary.

Gary poked his tousled head out of his tent.

'I can't find Batty!' Mandy gasped.

'It's OK,' he said sleepily. He unzipped the entrance to his tent. 'He's in here with me. I reckon he wanted to come in and keep warm!'

'Bats!' Mandy scolded. 'At this rate you'll never be fit to take care of yourself. And I'll never be able to get in touch with Hilda and tell her what a great wombat you are!'

Batty nuzzled close and she instantly forgave him. He was so sweet, so trusting, that she constantly had to force herself to remember their aim. 'It's the freedom of the forest for you, old boy!' she reminded him. 'Tonight we try again!'

And they did. Monday, Tuesday, Wednesday; before breakfast, after supper, they camped all week on the hill to train the wombat.

'I *think* he's getting the idea,' Mandy reported to her mum and dad by the middle of the week. Gary was in the shower, washing off excavation dirt. She dried her hair, almost ready for school.

'Is he still lodging in the trailer?' Emily Hope took a close interest.

'During the day. But he does come out in the evening, like he did at Orchard Farm. We leave the trailer ramp down at dusk, and he potters about all night long. We hear him snuffling around by the tent flaps.

'Has he started digging for himself?' Her mum spread marmalade on her toast.

'No, but he did go into one of our burrows and stayed there quite a long time. That was last night. He even took in some pieces of bark. He carries them in his mouth.'

'Good; that's progress at any rate.' She gave a satisfied nod. 'I'll give you a lift into school this morning,' she offered. 'I have to drive into town to see Cuddles, Vicki Jackson's echidna.'

'Cuddles?' Mandy laughed. Echidnas, or spiny anteaters, were like small porcupines, covered in spikes.

Mrs Hope nodded. 'It's Vicki's little joke, I suppose.'

They finished getting ready and set off together. 'So you think Batty's getting the idea?' Mandy sat in the Landcruiser between Gary and her mum. It was a brilliant blue January day.

'Yes, give him another few days to get used to his freedom. I expect it'll take a while, but in the end I'm sure you'll get there.'

'Good.' Mandy gazed down at her lap. Her wombat book lay open on her knee. ' "Wombats are easily kept in captivity," ' she read. ' "They have few natural enemies in the wild, but have suffered greatly at the hands of man. However, they make amusing and affectionate pets. One is reported to have lived for twenty-six years." '

'Wow!' Gary considered this. 'That means that old Bats still has a few years left in him.'

Mandy nodded. She had to shake off the old feeling of wanting to keep hold of Batty. She'd grown too fond of him, and had to remind herself that the wild was where he belonged. She looked up and straight ahead down the twisting road. 'Tonight!' she announced. 'I have this feeling that tonight is going to be the night when Batty digs his first burrow!'

'You were right! Look at that!' Gary breathed. He'd dimmed the torch to let the wombat dig undisturbed. He and Mandy had crept out of their tents to the sound of soil being scraped thick and fast. It was almost midnight. Batty was hard at work.

'I can't see him. I can only see the soil moving!' Mandy peered through the darkness.

He was thrusting it out of a hole between the thick, twisted roots of the acacia tree.

'Here he comes!' Gary pointed to the sight of Batty's broad backside and short hind legs emerging from the burrow. Soil was piled up to right and left. Batty sat down exhausted at the entrance. He twitched his blunt nose and shook his whiskers.

Mandy felt a surge of triumph. 'He did it! He dug himself a home!'

Gary held on to her. 'Shh! Better not distract him. How long do you reckon the tunnel is?'

'Who knows? It could be three to five metres, according to the book.'

'Hey look, now he's going after bits of bark. He's making a good job of things!'

They watched Batty trot off and come back with lining for his burrow. Moonlight gleamed silver on his thick, rough coat. He went off again, further this time. Soon a small pile of dry bark lay at the entrance to the burrow. Mandy and Gary squatted down and watched patiently.

After about half an hour, Batty must have decided he'd gathered enough. He began to plod inside his tunnel carrying one piece at a time, reappearing a minute or two later, his mouth empty.

'What do you reckon?' Gary asked. His face was drained of colour by the moonlight.

'Let's see if he goes back to the trailer to sleep, or if he uses his nest!' She hardly dared to breathe. They crouched in the deepest shadows of the tree and kept their fingers firmly crossed.

At last Batty seemed satisfied. He'd taken in his last piece of bark. But would he come out of the burrow and retreat to the comfort of the trailer as usual? They waited; two minutes, five, then ten. There was no sign of the wombat.

Gary turned to Mandy. 'What do you reckon?'

'I reckon he's tucked up snug and fast asleep in there!'

'Wow!' Gary heaved a satisfied sigh.

'Now he can get food *and* make a shelter!'

The hillside was peaceful. The clear creek bubbled and swirled between its banks, a night bird gave a high, fluting call. At last they crawled into their tents, happy that Batty had learned the basics. Soon he would be living like any other natural animal. He wouldn't need them any more, not once he was safely back in the wild.

Nine

Next morning, a Saturday, Mandy woke to the loud, laughing call of a kookaburra perched high in the acacia tree. Dawn had scarcely broken. Inside her cosy tent she snuggled deeper into her sleeping-bag. Their late night had made her extra sleepy, and today there was no need to get up for school. 'One more hour,' she promised herself. 'Then I'll get up and see what Bats is up to.'

But the kookaburra kept on calling. His cry echoed up and down the hillside. All hope of going back to sleep soon fled; she was wide awake. The grey light filtered into the tent, the creek splashed and gurgled over its rocky bed. 'Thanks a lot!' Mandy grumbled at the noisy bird. 'I guess you're my friendly morning alarm call!'

She unzipped her sleeping-bag and slowly crawled out of the tent. The kookaburra laughed high in the tree, then flapped off to annoy someone else. Mandy watched him rise and fly over the misty hilltop. She stretched, glanced at Gary's quiet tent, and went to splash her face in the cold stream. 'Now, Batty,' she said to herself, 'it's time you were up and foraging for breakfast.' She wandered to the entrance of the newly dug tunnel.

It seemed he had beaten her to it. As she crouched to investigate the burrow, she saw telltale signs of the wombat's early rising. There was freshly scraped earth by the entrance, some half-eaten roots, and a few metres away a new shallow hollow which Batty had worked on since last night. He'd been scraping away at his sunbathing spot, ready for an after-breakfast snooze.

But where was he now? Mandy decided to try and track him down. 'You're not the only one who gets up at the crack of dawn,' she murmured, following a flattened trail through some long dry grass towards the old trailer. She felt proud of him, despite her grumbles. She saw that their own patience was beginning to pay off. Everything was going according to plan, Batty's lessons in survival were almost complete.

Glancing into the empty trailer, Mandy continued up the hill. Batty's morning trail showed that he was growing daring. He'd ventured on to new territory, into the bush and scrubland at the top of the hill. A thorny bush scraped against her leg; something moved unseen in the shadow of a large boulder. Mandy felt her senses grow suddenly alert, on the lookout for the wombat in his new, natural surroundings.

At last she spotted him. He'd stopped by a small gum tree for a nibble at the tender inner bark. He was so busy eating that he didn't notice her squat down in the grass to watch. Mandy smiled. Trust Bats to find a tasty morsel for his breakfast. He stuffed his cheeks full to bursting, tore at the soft bark with his sharp claws and pushed it into his mouth.

As Mandy watched, her smile turned to a small frown. Batty's sheltered life with Hilda had made him too trusting, she realised.

Batty was in seventh heaven, munching, sighing, picking at the bark at the base of the tree. He had his broad back towards a small clearing. Mandy watched from the shelter of the grass. Though he was a long way from safety, maybe three hundred metres up the hill from his burrow, he acted as if he didn't have a care in the world.

The first strange thing Mandy noticed was a tiny movement in the long grass behind the gum tree. Batty didn't react. Maybe he didn't even see it. He munched on, senses dulled by his feast of bark. She told herself it was nothing; an echidna shuffling out of its night-time shelter into the dewy air, perhaps. Whatever it was, it was well camouflaged. Minutes passed. Mandy watched a family of brown rabbits emerge from a small burrow and begin their morning grooming. Then there was another movement in the grass, quick and stealthy. The rabbits shot back into hiding.

This time Batty did look up. But he was slow. He wouldn't have stood a chance if Mandy hadn't sprung to her feet with a yell. 'Dingo!' Her shout split the silence. 'Batty, watch out!'

She saw the dangerous streak of yellow, the terrible snapping, snarling jaws as the wild dog curled back its lips and bounded into the clearing.

Batty looked up, puzzled. He had no chance to move; the hunter was almost upon him.

Without a thought for her own safety, Mandy charged to the rescue. She covered the ground with her long legs, yelling, hoping to distract the dingo from its prey, as she'd once seen Graham do when he showed her the wild wombats on Peppermint Hill.

The dog swerved off course and stopped, ears pricked. She looked Mandy in the eye. Was it right that dingoes avoided humans? Mandy prayed it was true. She fixed the dingo with her stare, advanced slowly, intent on getting between her and poor old Batty, who had backed against the gum tree and was crouched there trembling.

It was a battle of nerves. Who would give way? Mandy didn't break her gaze. Her whole body shook, her throat was dry, but she edged forward, a human barrier between the two animals. At last the dingo's mouth closed over her bared teeth, she dropped her head and slunk off, deprived of her prey . . . for now.

Mandy took a deep breath. She needed to steady her nerves. Then she turned to Batty. 'See!' she scolded. 'That's what happens when you don't keep a lookout! And you know you're miles away from your burrow!'

Batty blinked and waddled towards her. She bent to stroke him. 'Bats, you were nearly a goner!'

He nuzzled her fingers.

She relented. 'Oh, it's OK showing off, digging your own home,' she murmured. She took the wombat into her arms to carry him back to his burrow. 'It's all very well,' she told him, 'but it's a big world out here and you wombats have to learn to stick up for yourselves.' She talked herself calm before she went to Gary's tent and told him about Batty's close shave.

He listened gravely. 'What can we do? If Bats doesn't see danger for himself, I don't reckon there's any lessons we can give him to teach him that!'

They watched Batty settle into a short nap in the early sun. When he woke, he stretched, sniffed around and munched a couple of roots before retiring for the day to his new burrow in the bank of the stream.

'How do you teach a wombat self-defence?' she asked her mum when she and Gary went down to the house for their own breakfast.

'Hmm, I don't think you can.' Emily Hope agreed with Gary. 'Batty's never going to be a black belt in karate, if that's what you mean. Wombats aren't aggressive animals at the best of times, and that's that, I'm afraid.'

Mandy nodded. It was hard to accept, but Batty would have to take his own chances from now on. She wouldn't always be around to protect him. Their job was nearly done.

That afternoon, Mandy gave up a chance to go to the beach with her mum, dad and Katie Browne. Instead, she stayed at home to write her letter to Hilda. She reported on Batty's training programme. 'We've taught him how to make his own burrow,' she wrote. 'And now we think he's ready to fend for himself. One of these nights, Dad says he'll wander off to dig a new one and that will be it. He'll be off into the wild again. Don't worry, he'll have a happy life, free to roam.'

She wanted to cheer Hilda up. But as she sealed the envelope and wrote the Sydney address, Mandy didn't feel so sure. Memories of Batty's puzzled face as the dingo attacked had stayed with her. He hadn't recognised the danger. Any animal who'd been wild since birth would have learned this the hard way. Would Batty ever regain the instinct to survive out there? This thought brought a frown to her face as she went into the yard, picked up her bike, and cycled to the postbox in Mitchell to post Hilda's letter.

That night, in an unexpected way, the problem of trying to teach Batty the art of self-defence was taken out of their hands.

After the sun had set, Mandy and Gary spent a pleasant hour watching the wombat potter in the shelter of the old acacia tree. His morning brush with danger seemed forgotten, as he trudged the worn pathways between tents and burrow. He searched out a juicy root here, accepted a titbit of bark there, seeming especially friendly, Mandy thought. Gary said she was imagining things; Batty was his same old shambling, easy-going self, he said.

'No, look, he's trying to tell us something!' Mandy insisted. Batty rested his head against her knees, staring up into her face. She scratched the top of his flat head.

'Says you!' Gary sat with his feet in the creek, cooling down.

But when Bats wandered across and poked his blunt nose against his face, even Gary admitted that the wombat was definitely up to something. 'Steady on, mate!' He pushed him away in a play-fight and ended up tickling him.

Mandy watched with a smile. Her mum came up quietly and sat with them, checking that they had all they needed for another night under canvas. 'He's certainly getting more adventurous,' she commented. Batty's familiar back view climbed high on the hillside.

'Yes.' Mandy sighed.

'Worse luck, eh?' Emily Hope squeezed her daughter's hand. 'Get a good night's sleep,' she told them both. 'And if I were you, I wouldn't wait up for the wanderer to return!' She scanned the empty hillside. 'I reckon he's gone walkabout and won't be back until morning.'

Reluctantly Mandy and Gary took to their tents. Mrs Hope was right; Batty's night-time jaunt was a long one. They didn't hear him come back, though by now they were alert to every sound. 'No, Bats isn't coming home tonight,'

Mandy said to herself as she finally settled down to sleep.

And he wasn't home when dawn broke, or during breakfast, which Adam Hope brought up for them. Everyone kept a lookout. Batty was late back, but Mandy tried not to worry. After all, this was the way it was meant to be. One night, Batty would wander off and dig himself a fresh burrow. She'd always known that. Now that it had happened, she had no reason to fret. But she felt empty. She would miss his solid, stumpy figure and their daily routine of teaching him how to survive.

'I reckon you were right.' Gary came alongside. They stood together, gazing at Batty's first attempts to build his own home. The ground under the acacia tree was scraped bare, and the entrance to his own first burrow looked lonely and empty.

'How come?' Mandy gazed on.

'Bats *was* trying to say something.'

She nodded. 'It felt like goodbye.'

'I reckon,' he said quietly.

Neither could say any more. The sun was high in the sky. It was Sunday, a day for the beach.

* * *

Gary soon went home, promising to meet up with Mandy later.

Down at the house, Adam Hope was enjoying a swim and Emily Hope was reading in the shade of the veranda. Mandy wandered in and out like a lost soul. She smiled briefly when Katie and Graham arrived for lunch, but her heart wasn't in the friendly chatter.

Graham, kind as ever, noticed. 'I hear you're working on old Bats to get him back into the wild?' he asked cheerfully.

Katie was more up-to-date. 'Your dad tells me the wombat took off last night,' she said matter of factly. 'About time too, the old villain!' She gave a quick grin. 'You bet he's tucked up in some new burrow, no worries!'

'I hope so.' Quickly Mandy told Katie about the episode with the hungry dingo.

Katie nodded and considered this. 'Do you fancy making a quick recce?' She sprang to her feet.

'A what?'

'A recce. A look up the hill. We can soon find out if the dingo has had another go at him!'

Mandy swallowed then nodded. 'OK.' It was better to know for sure than to spend her time wondering. She went after their nurse towards the creek, working hard to keep up with her long stride. Down in the yard, her mum, dad and Graham sat by the pool, taking things easy after their meal.

'What exactly are we looking for?' Mandy gasped. She'd finally caught up with Katie as they came to the brow of the hill.

'Wombat tracks. New digging. There aren't any others round here, I reckon.' Katie stood, one foot resting on a boulder. She scanned the downward slope of the hill.

'No, I haven't seen any besides Batty,' Mandy agreed. 'And I'm sure Gary and I would have seen or heard them while we were camping out.'

'So it stands to reason that any new burrow we find belongs to old Bats?'

Mandy nodded.

'Right then, you go that way. I'll try this ridge here.'

Mandy was happy to take orders. Even if they didn't manage to find where Batty had holed up, it was good to be out looking. She was grateful that Katie had understood how much he meant to her. If only she could find out that he was safe; that was all she needed to know.

She followed Katie's instructions, treading carefully between bushes, looking for telltale hollows and piles of loose earth.

They searched for ten minutes, then met up again. 'Anything?' Katie asked. She shaded her eyes from the sun with her hand. Her short, corn-coloured hair stuck to her neck in the midday heat.

'No.' Mandy hadn't come across anything bigger than a lizard basking on a flat rock.

'Let's try down towards that gully.' Katie headed into a wilder landscape of dark yellow rocks and thorny bushes. This time the two of them stuck together.

'What's that?' Mandy had spotted something. It was freshly dug earth, still damp, lying on the dry surface close to the stump of a wizened tree; ideal wombat territory. Her hopes rose.

Katie nodded. 'Good on you.' They half ran towards the spot. Sure enough, the soil was piled by the entrance to a new burrow, just wide and tall enough for a wombat's bulky frame.

'Great!' Mandy could hardly contain her excitement. 'Good old Batty!' She longed to rush forward and check that the burrow was occupied.

But Katie held her back. 'Wait!'

Mandy paused and watched her drop on one knee. 'What is it?'

She prodded the earth with her fingertips. 'Looks like there's been a scrap here.' She sounded serious.

'Where?' Mandy dropped beside her. She reached out her hand to feel the scuffed marks close to the entrance to the burrow. Sharp claws had torn through the soil and uprooted clumps of grass. Heavy bodies had rolled, fur caught in the thorn bushes. Thick dark fur, greyish-brown, and a tuft of bright orange-yellow hair.

'Oh!' Mandy lifted her fingers towards her face. She rubbed her thumb against them. The sticky, red smears made her stomach turn. 'It's blood!' she gasped.

Katie gave one sharp nod. Her own fingers were stained dark crimson.

'Batty!' Mandy crawled to the burrow and called softly, then more urgently. 'Bats, here, boy!'

They both knew it was useless. The burrow was empty.

Then Katie spotted another patch of blood. It formed a trail, leading away from the burrow, across stretches of flattened grass, ending in the shadowy bottom of the gully on stony, hard ground. Mandy shivered. 'Did you hear that?'

'No, what?'

'A kind of whine.'

Katie stood up straight. 'This is where the trail goes dead.'

'Listen, there it is again. More of a howl. Did you hear?'

This time Katie nodded. 'Dingo.'

The word sent shivers through Mandy from head to toe.

'Come on.' Katie helped her to her feet. She looked deadly serious. 'Sorry, kid,' she said gently. Then she led the way out of the gully, over the hill, back to Mitchell Gap.

Ten

There was no meeting up with the gang on the beach later that day. Mandy phoned Gary to tell him the bad news; Batty had been in a fight with the dingo. Now there was no sign of him.

He came straight over to Mitchell Gap. His cheerful laid-back manner had gone, but he tried his best to hide how upset he felt.

'Sorry to hear about Batty,' Adam Hope told him, giving him a pat on the shoulder. 'But don't blame yourselves. You did all you could.'

Gary nodded, blushed and turned away. 'Where did the fight happen?' he asked Mandy.

She took him up to the spot, past the farm

trailer where Batty had safely lodged, over the brow of the hill to the unfriendly rocky spot where they'd discovered the final patches of blood.

'At least he put up a fight,' Gary said. He stood, hands in the pockets of his shorts, head hanging.

In their own minds they forced themselves to confront Batty's last moments.

'I wonder where the dingo is now.' Mandy pictured her roaming the lonely slopes, around the edges of the town. There was a long pause. 'You know, I can't help hoping . . . I mean, I know it's not likely, but . . .' She stopped in mid-sentence and stared at him.

Gary picked her up right away. 'You want to keep on looking?'

She nodded quickly. 'We don't know for sure, do we?' Katie had assumed the worst; the story of a wombat caught in the open and attacked by a dingo usually had only one ending. 'The thing is, we'd never forgive ourselves if poor Batty is lying injured somewhere!'

The tiny hope was enough to spur them on. As teatime passed and evening drew in, Gary and Mandy scoured the far side of the hill. They climbed rocks and peered down crevices, they beat their way through thorn bushes with stout sticks. Adam Hope came to see what they were up to. He went home shaking his head. Just before sunset, Emily Hope called them in for a break. She gave them tea and sandwiches.

'Any luck?' She sat opposite them at the kitchen table. Outside, cicadas filled the evening air with their scratching chorus.

Gary shook his head. 'Nah, we didn't find a thing.'

'Maybe that's good,' Mandy put in. 'It might mean Batty managed to get clear of the dingo somehow . . . if it *was* a dingo.'

'If it *was* Batty,' Gary added.

Mrs Hope said nothing. It was obvious she thought they were fooling themselves.

Mandy finished her tea first and stood up, ready to go back up the hill to carry on with their search.

'I'd like you home before it gets dark,' her mum reminded them. 'It's not a good idea to be out there in the bush with a dingo roaming the area.'

They promised, and set out for one last try to find out exactly what had become of Batty.

'Just one little sign!' Mandy pleaded, as they reached the brow of the hill, the border between the safety of Mitchell Gap and the unknown dangers of the bush. All they needed was one fresh wombat track, a pile of half-chewed roots, a new burrow.

But the hillside yielded no clues. Only the whining cry of a dingo chilled the air, and the eerie sense that bright, fierce, amber eyes followed them wherever they went.

Dusk fell. Wearily Mandy and Gary gave up the search and headed home.

'Now we'll never know,' she admitted. For the last time they went to check the entrance to the burrow which she and Katie had discovered earlier that afternoon. In the red rays of the setting sun, they crouched to examine the site of Batty's struggle. The heat had dried the bloodstains dark brown, the wind had blown the torn fur from the thorns. Gently Mandy called Batty's name. Her voice echoed. They stood up, listened to the silence, and went home.

Next morning at breakfast, Adam Hope looked on anxiously as Mandy sat in her dressing-gown and fiddled with the spoon in her full bowl of cereal. 'Eat something,' he suggested. 'It'll help make you feel better.'

Her mum came into the kitchen from the surgery. She'd been out in the residential unit, checking a cat that had been brought in a couple of days earlier, suffering from a snake bite. Luckily, the owner had been able to bring in the snake as well, and they'd soon found the antidote. Now the cat was progressing well.

'Did I hear the phone ring?' Mrs Hope asked, brisk and busy in her crisp white coat.

Mandy nodded. She'd taken the message, which had been rerouted from the empty surgery into the house. 'Merv rang to say that one of his customer's blueheelers has gone down with slug-bait poisoning. He's going to bring him straight over here before he begins his deliveries. The owner has a broken ankle and can't drive.'

Emily Hope nodded. Blueheelers were great dogs; an outdoor Australian breed, something like Staffordshire bull terriers back home. 'I expect he'll need his stomach pumped out, then he'll be fine!' She looked at Mandy sitting hunched over her cereal bowl. 'Are you going to get ready for school?' she prompted.

'Yes. I've got loads of time.' She'd hardly slept during the night, and now she felt weighed down, nothing like her usual bright self. When she and Gary had finally parted, after Abbie Simpson had driven over to pick him up, they'd vowed not to mention Batty when they met up at school next day. They said they wanted to go on as normal, going to the beach, helping in the surgery, having a laugh. But she didn't feel normal. She would have to go through the motions of lessons, of chatting with Julie and Suzi about this and that. But she'd just be covering up.

Mandy sighed, gave up on her breakfast, and tried to look as if she could cope. She noticed her mum and dad exchange worried looks as she went off to her room to change into her school uniform.

Ready, and still with time to kill, she wandered out into the yard. She'd heard her dad drive off in the Landcruiser, and now she saw Merv's van arrive. She watched as he let Herbie jump out, ahead of Merv himself. The storekeeper leaned inside the van, then carried the collapsed blueheeler up the shallow wooden steps into the surgery.

Normally Mandy would have been in there with him, eager to lend a hand. But this morning she turned away and walked up the hill. She crossed the creek, looking for a quiet moment before she finally picked up her bike and headed for school.

Something took her towards the old acacia tree. Maybe she was hoping for a rare glimpse of the family of platypuses that lived in the bank by the stream. Maybe she just wanted to dream of seeing Batty in his old, safe haunt. She crouched by the gnarled roots and gazed at the old workings; the piles of dry earth, the scooped out hollows, their man-made efforts to teach the old wombat new tricks.

Somehow the sight cheered her. It was true Batty had gone away from here and met only danger. It was true that she and Gary would probably never know what had happened to him in the end. But, as she studied the half-made tunnels and little piles of bark, she knew that her dad was right; they had done their very best.

Just then, she felt rather than saw a movement on the hill. There was a scuffling and a shuffling through the grass. Something moved slowly towards her. 'No!' she thought. She bit her lip and waited, sitting still as a stone. A shape emerged, limping unsteadily towards her: Batty. He struggled down the slope. One hind leg had a bad gash, one round ear was torn. But he kept going.

Mandy was rooted to the spot. 'Bats!' She opened her arms to greet him. He stumbled into them and she closed them round him. 'Oh, Bats, it's you!' she sobbed. 'You brave, brave thing!'

She took him gently to the old trailer and made him stay there. 'Don't move! I'll be right back.' She knew he would be safe, and she didn't want to risk carrying him all the way down to the surgery. Then she ran down the hill, splashed through the creek, leaped over rocks into the yard at Mitchell Gap, yelling for her mum to come quick.

Merv came out to see what the noise was about. 'Cut it out!' he barked when he saw Mandy careering across the yard. 'She's busy with the blueheeler. We've got to get his stomach pumped clear!'

Mandy stopped short. She was breathless, her hair tumbled over her face, as she gabbled and pointed. Then she caught sight of Katie cycling in through the gate. She ran to her with the news.

'Katie, come quick! Batty's here! He is! He's been injured, but he's still alive! You've got to come, quick as you can!'

The nurse dropped her bike and ran inside for her medical bag. She raced up the hill after Mandy. They found Batty curled in the straw in the trailer, patiently waiting. It must have taken all his strength to get back to Mitchell Gap. Now he could only tremble and pant, as Katie climbed into the trailer to examine him.

Mandy clambered up after her. She watched as the nurse felt gently round the jagged gash on Batty's hind leg.

'Not broken,' Katie confirmed. 'Could be infected though.' She took the wombat's temperature. 'Yes, he's got a fever. We'll need to clean the wounds.' She asked Mandy to hold Batty steady while she poured antiseptic lotion on to clean gauze. She worked quickly and calmly.

'Will he need stitches?' Mandy asked.

'Not at this stage. The wound is already healing over, see. And this one on his ear won't come to any harm. It'll just make him look a bit strange, won't it, old mate?' She winked. 'Everyone will know he's been in the wars from now on.'

'But he's going to be all right?' Mandy sat on the floor of the trailer, Batty's heavy head resting in her lap. 'Will we have to take him down to the surgery?'

'Best not,' Katie said. She closed her bag and gave Batty one last check over. 'We don't want to undo all your good work by making a pet of him all over again.'

'Are you sure he'll be OK if we leave him out here?' She looked anxiously at the wound on his leg.

'He's tougher than he looks!' Katie reminded her.

As if to prove it, Batty struggled to his feet. He nosed his way through the straw, but finding nothing to eat, he headed for the ramp and trundled slowly down. Katie put a warning hand on Mandy's arm. 'No, don't help. Let him do it for himself!'

He made it to ground level, and immediately shuffled off after fresh grass roots. Soon he was chewing happily.

'He's amazing!' Mandy breathed.

'Now let's see!' Katie leaned both arms on the side of the trailer. With their grandstand view they watched what the wombat would do next.

He finished chewing. He looked round and cocked his head at them. Then he ambled off, letting the injured leg only gently touch the ground as he went. It gave him an odd, lopsided walk.

Mandy smiled. 'I wonder what happened?' She pictured Batty scrapping for all he was worth against the dingo, turning and charging with all his weight, avoiding the snapping jaws. He'd given as good as he got.

'Who knows? Maybe the dingo didn't reckon on a fight. Maybe she got distracted by some easier prey.' Katie shrugged. 'At least we know now that Bats can well and truly take care of himself. That dingo must have felt like she'd gone a couple of rounds with a heavyweight boxing champion!'

Mandy heaved a deep sigh, watching intently as Batty sniffed out one of his old tracks. He followed it, up to the entrance of his own first burrow in the bank of the stream. He stopped, turned his head this way and that. Was it good enough, now that he'd learned to do the job properly? Was it deep enough, and properly lined with bark? He seemed to say yes, it would do for him to rest up and get over his injury. Giving a little grunt, he glanced back at Mandy and Katie, then shuffled forward. With a pull and a tug he squeezed his rear end into the burrow, and was gone.

'Home again!' Katie picked up her bag and vaulted the side of the trailer. She glanced up at Mandy. 'Hey, aren't you supposed to be at school?'

Mandy remembered the time. 'Oh no!' She shot down the hill, flicking straw from her uniform, trying desperately to scrape her hair into a neat ponytail. In the yard, she bumped into her mum and Merv.

'Mum, Batty escaped the dingo! He's back. He's holed up by the creek. He is!' She saw the disbelieving smile vanish from Emily Hope's face. 'Ask Katie. I've got to dash!'

She sped on her bike into Eurabbie, over the tree-lined hills, along the winding bushland tracks. The last stretch was downhill all the way. She found Gary hanging about by the gate, anxiously looking out for her. 'He's back!' she yelled at the top of her voice. She screeched to a halt. 'Batty came home!'

Other kids looked at her strangely. She had straw in her hair, her words tumbled out. She filled in the details as she and Gary headed for their classroom.

'You're telling me he's chosen Mitchell Gap as his full-time home?' He swung his bag on to his desk. Mrs Bertram called for silence to begin the register. 'I thought the idea was to get him back into the wild?'

Mandy nodded. 'It is,' she whispered. 'The creek is what he likes best, and it's not as if he's asking us to look after him, is it? He's living *close* to civilisation, not actually *in* it!'

'No,' he agreed. 'It's like he tried the open bush, and he found it wasn't for him.' He broke off the whispered conversation to answer his name.

'Right!' Mandy's face had spread into a wide grin. 'He had a taste of it and look what happened. A dingo, that's what. So he headed straight back to where he knew he'd be safe!'

Wait till I write again to tell Hilda! she thought. This was the best of all possible solutions. If Batty stayed put and made the creek his permanent home, the dingo would keep her distance and he'd be safe from any future attack. Better still, she and Gary would be able to go up and have a chat with him any time they felt like it.

'Pretty smart.' Gary was impressed. Good old Batty had found his way back to Mitchell Gap for treatment.

As Mandy gathered her schoolbooks for her first lesson, she thought of Batty snuggled up warm and cosy in the burrow on the hill. 'Yes,' she agreed. 'I reckon Mitchell Gap is as wild as this wombat wants to be!'

*If you've enjoyed this Animal Ark story,
you'll love . . .*

LUCY DANIELS

Roo

– *on the* –

Rock

Here is the first chapter.

One

Mandy Hope sat listening to Katie Browne who was whistling as she drove. She yawned, wishing that the journey was over. The red sun was low in the sky. It was late in a hot March day at the end of a long, dry Australian summer.

Katie swerved to avoid a gang of little hare wallabies that ran like the wind along the side of the rough road. Heads up, forelegs dangling, they seemed to be whistling back at her.

Mandy sat in the back of the powerful Landcruiser with her friend, Gary Simpson. They watched the wallabies dash ahead, then dart back on their tracks, disappearing into the bush as fast as they'd come. Mandy held her breath. The beautiful creatures, with their large, pointed ears and dark eyes, seemed to be running straight into danger.

'You Aussies are only twenty-five million years behind the times!' Adam Hope wisecracked at Katie, the nurse at Mitchell Gap Veterinary Centre.

Katie slowed down to take a bend and began to climb the hill that would take them through the small town of Mitchell to Mandy's home, the vets' practice at Mitchell Gap which was run by her mother and father. 'So how come, according to you we're past our sell-by date?' Katie challenged Mandy's dad.

Half-dozing in the back of the car, Mandy grinned as she listened to their nurse stand up to him.

'Because!' He waved his arms at the mountainous countryside. 'For a start, the sea cut you off from the rest of the world at least sixty million years ago. And secondly, you have over a hundred species of that strange type of mammal, the marsupial!' He put on a jokey voice; a kind of studious, know-it-all tone.

'Ignore him!' Mandy whispered to Gary. She

shifted to get comfortable. They'd been driving all day, home from Melbourne Zoo. Katie had organised the four-day trip to give them close-up views of koalas and flying squirrels, emus, black swans and lyre birds, together with funnel-web spiders, crocodiles and snakes. Mandy had loved every minute; especially the nursery section which housed the orphan joeys and wallabies. But now she would be glad to get home to their house by the freshwater creek, with its shady veranda and cool swimming-pool. In fact, she could hardly wait.

'So?' Katie took another bend. The wallabies reappeared out of nowhere and raced alongside.

Mandy flinched and looked the other way.

'So, in Europe and North America, marsupials have been extinct for twenty-five million years!' Mr Hope declared. 'Like I said, you're behind the times. Where else would you find over a hundred species of animals that still tuck their babies into a pocket and lug them round with them wherever they go?'

Mandy saw the wallabies veer off again. She relaxed and rested her head back against the seat. 'I think that's neat! Ready-made pockets!' she grinned. She loved the way Nature solved problems like how to carry your young.

Her dad turned with a wink. 'You would! Whose side are you on?'

'Katie's.'

'Traitor! Take the kookaburra, for instance.' Mr Hope went on.

'A kookaburra isn't a marsupial,' Mandy pointed out. 'It's a bird!'

'I know that. I'm just using it as another example of the crazy animals over here. Here you have a kingfisher which can't fish. So what does he do? He eats rats and reptiles instead!'

'We *like* kookaburras, don't we, Katie?' Mandy had grown used to the bird's weird cry during her five months in Australia. One woke them each morning, calling from the acacia tree behind the house.

'It sounds like a donkey laughing,' her dad complained. 'I can't get my beauty sleep because of that jackass racket!'

'Not for much longer,' Gary reminded him. The trip to Melbourne Zoo had been one last Australian treat for Mandy and her dad. In a month's time, the Hopes would pack up and go back to England.

Mandy sighed. Home to Animal Ark, to Gran

and Grandad Hope and all her friends in Welford, the small village in Yorkshire where the Hopes lived. They would have to leave this vast, wonderful, colourful country behind.

Adam Hope kept the argument going. He wanted to make sure that Katie didn't doze at the wheel. 'And where else in the world would you find squirrels that fly?'

'New Guinea,' Mandy chipped in quietly.

'Hmph. And mammals that lay eggs?'

She knew that he meant the platypus; another Australian curiosity, with its duck-shaped bill and otter's tail.

'*And* 2000 kilometres of coral reef with millions of tropical fish? *And* the biggest rock on earth?' Gary added proudly. He told them about Ayers Rock, in the dead centre of Australia. 'It's about eight kilometres if you walk right round it, and it's 350-odd metres high; one single rock slap in the middle of the desert!'

'Sacred place for the Aborigines,' Katie said softly; 'I'll take you there next time you come.' She pulled at the wheel to avoid a spiny echidna which trundled across the road in front of them. They swerved back on to the road, just missing a battered metal sign. 'If you have a couple of weeks to spare, that is.'

Mandy read the notice: 'Watch Out For Kangaroos.' She leaned forward. 'Can you slow down a bit, Katie?' She was suddenly on the alert as she scanned the hillside for any sign of the roos.

'If I slow down any more, we might as well get out and walk the rest of the way!' Katie laughed. She tucked into the side, as another car came towards them on the single-track road. It roared by in a cloud of dust.

'How much further?' Mandy asked.

'Not far. About twenty kilometres to Mitchell, and then just five or six to the Gap.' Katie ran the back of her hand across her forehead, then grasped the steering-wheel once more.

'Want me to take over?' Adam Hope asked. They'd shared the driving on the long trip back from Melbourne.

She nodded and pulled off the road on to a rocky verge. 'Please. I'm whacked!'

They changed places, while Mandy and Gary peered into the valley ahead. 'Look, I can see the ocean!' Gary pointed to the right. Way in the distance there was a hazy blue line.

'I bet you can't wait to get there!' Mandy grinned at him. She knew Gary was surf-mad. He was in training for the junior boogie boarding championship next summer. It was impossible to keep him away from the beach and the high, rolling waves. Yet for four days he'd given up the surf and his board to come to the zoo.

'I could never drag him away for that long!' his mum, Abbie Simpson, had said, laughing.

His dad, Don, had winked and said nothing.

Since Mandy had arrived in Eurabbie Bay, Gary had discovered a new interest in animals, Don Simpson often teased. Now they didn't know if he would follow his dad's footsteps into the family swimming-pool business or if he would go to college and study to be a vet.

Mandy and Gary were best friends. He had shown her how to enjoy the outdoor life in Australia. She was a good boogie-boarder, thanks to Gary's coaching. It was one of the things she would miss when she went home to Welford.

Soon, with her dad in the driving seat for the final run into Eurabbie Bay, they were on their way again. Gary spotted the small town of

Mitchell, nestled between two tree-covered hills, and beyond that, way down on the distant coast, the bigger town of Eurabbie itself. 'Hey, my uncle lives up here some place,' he told them.

'I never knew you had an uncle!' Mandy was surprised. He never showed up at any of the Simpsons' barbecues by the side of their pool at Waratarah, their posh house overlooking Eurabbie Bay.

'No. It's my dad's brother, Uncle Art. We don't talk about him!' Gary went red and laughed it off. 'Forget I mentioned him!' He pushed his wavy sun-bleached hair back from his tanned face.

The car swayed and lurched over the rough road. 'Why?' Mandy hadn't pictured the Simpsons with a dark secret. Don and Abbie Simpson seemed ultra-respectable.

'We just don't have much to do with him.' Gary shrugged. 'They had a row about money when my grandpa died. He's got some farm or other up here. A couple of sheep, a goat, you know . . .' He trailed off again.

Mandy sighed. 'Here's me thinking you had a bank robber for an uncle, or something exciting like that!'

'Sorry, no. It's just boring old Uncle Art, with his beehives and his honey!' Gary hung on to the roll-bar as the Landcruiser tilted and dipped down a deep hole in the road.

'So why don't they make up the quarrel, then he could come over to Waratarah to visit?'

'I dunno. He reckons he doesn't have time.' Gary shuffled in his seat and stared out at the gum trees which lined the road ahead.

Mandy frowned. 'How can a couple of sheep, a goat and a beehive take up *all* his time?'

'Mandy!' Adam Hope gave her a warning glance. He changed the subject. 'Do I spy a buster gathering out at sea?'

They all craned their necks to see a tiny cloud forming on the horizon. The weekly storms would begin almost without warning; a puff or two of cloud, a couple of gusts of wind, then sudden downpour.

'Nah!' Katie crossed her fingers. A buster would force them off the road for an hour or two. 'Please don't rain on us now!'

Another cloud swept into view. 'No, not now we're nearly home!' Mandy cried. She longed to get home to her mum, a cold shower, and all the latest news about the patients in their kennels at the back of the surgery.

'Yep!' Gary confirmed with a nod. 'That's a buster all right!'

It took their minds off his Uncle Art. Adam Hope put his foot on the accelerator and tried to make it home before the storm.

'Kangaroos, Dad; remember!' Mandy warned. She saw one or two hop steadily across the road ahead. When she looked harder, she saw there were lots of them around, in the bush and loping by the roadside.

'Evening's their time for heading to the high ridges,' Katie explained. 'Mobs of sixty or more roos will go up into the hills for the night. They follow a set path, regular as clockwork.' She told them that this was when the 'Watch Out For Kangaroos' warnings were especially important.

Mandy felt herself tense up again. Another car had zoomed past in the opposite direction, trying to beat the storm. And now someone came lurching up behind, almost bumper to bumper with their own car. He hooted his horn to make them get a move on. She turned and glared.

Gary leaned out of the window and looked up at the sky. The two small clouds had quickly gathered into a dark, angry mass that whipped across and hid the setting sun. Soon, the hills were in deep shadow. Big splashes of rain began to hit the windscreen. 'Here it comes!' he warned.

'Hang on, I'll just pull off the road here and let this chap through!' Mr Hope signalled and braked. But the road was too narrow, and it was too late for the impatient driver to beat the storm. The heavy, single splashes became a downpour. Rain battered on to the bonnets of the cars and turned their windscreens into waterfalls.

Soon, both Adam Hope and the other driver had to give in. They pulled into the side of the road together and sat under the gum trees, watching the road turn into a muddy, brown river.

'No one's going anywhere while this storm lasts,' Mr Hope said.

Mandy would have to wait a while for her home comforts. She stared out of the window at the blurred shapes of the poor wallabies. Further off, a herd of bigger kangaroos grazed miserably. There was nothing for it; they would have to wait for the buster to blow itself out.

Dear Reader

*I'm so pleased with the letters I have been receiving about **Animal Ark**. It seems there are lots of fans of the series, and I am very happy that so many people are enjoying the books.*

I especially enjoy reading your suggestions for new titles – so keep them coming!

Much love,

Lucy Daniels

KOALAS IN A CRISIS
Animal Ark in Australia, 16

Lucy Daniels

Mandy longs to meet her first koala and she's not disappointed when she visits the wildlife sanctuary.

But her joy turns to horror when she learns that the baby koalas and their babies are threatened.

Can Mandy save the koalas from starvation?

ROO ON THE ROCK
Animal Ark in Australia, 18

Lucy Daniels

Moonbeam is an orphaned baby kangaroo. He's too young to survive on his own – he'll have to be sent to a zoo.

But Mandy thinks wild animals should stay in the wild – she's not going to let this roo spend the rest of his life in captivity!

Can Mandy help Moonbeam escape?

ANIMAL ARK SERIES
LUCY DANIELS